Waiting for a "Pearl Harbor"

WAITING
FOR A
"PEARL HARBOR"

Japan Debates Defense

TETSUYA KATAOKA

HOOVER INSTITUTION PRESS
Stanford University, Stanford, California

The Hoover Institution on War, Revolution and Peace, founded at Stanford University in 1919 by the late President Herbert Hoover, is an interdisciplinary research center for advanced study on domestic and international affairs in the twentieth century. The views expressed in its publications are entirely those of the authors and do not necessarily reflect the views of the staff, officers, or Board of Overseers of the Hoover Institution.

Hoover Institution Publication 232

Designed by Elizabeth Gehman

For Barbara

Contents

Editor's Foreword

Readers of Prof. Tetsuya Kataoka's monograph will be challenged to reassess their views about the balance of power in East Asia as well as throughout the rest of the world. This study, which is bound to generate controversy in the United States and Japan, is timely because of a new dilemma that will confront the United States during the 1980s.

It is a well-known fact that American defense outlays, as compared with Soviet military expenditures, have declined steadily over the past two decades. The USSR not only achieved equivalence but indeed has overtaken the United States in certain categories of weaponry: more warships, strategic launchers, advanced missiles, and warheads. Furthermore, efforts by Washington to stop Moscow's geopolitical expansionism over the past quarter-century have been unsuccessful. The Soviet Union recently extended its sphere of influence in Vietnam, notably at the huge U.S.-built port of Camranh Bay, much to the consternation of the People's Republic of China and to the growing concern of Japan.

As the world balance of power continues to shift toward the USSR, regional configurations are likely to change. Throughout East Asia, such developments may well produce new and unintended consequences for major world powers like Japan.

How Japan responds to these circumstances will be of profound importance for the United States. From the viewpoint of a patriotic Japanese citizen, Professor Kataoka cogently argues that policymakers in Washington have failed to build a strong and durable partnership with Tokyo. By taking Japan for granted, so to speak, the United States has ignored at its peril new forces within that country that could react unilaterally to the changing balance of power in East Asia. How these forces will shape Japan's defense posture in the future and their implications for American foreign policy are the topics explored in this fascinating and provocative study, which is a welcome addition to the Hoover Institution's international studies series.

RICHARD F. STAAR

Hoover Institution   *Director of International Studies*

Foreword

Japan rearmed!

Here is a specter that sends chills down spines on both shores of the Pacific.

In those beautiful islands of the Far East, millions of Japanese cling to the conviction that the greatest mistake they ever made was to let their government fall into the hands of militarists in the 1930s. They would regard a recurrence as nothing less than flirtation with another national disaster.

For Americans with Pearl Harbor and the ensuing four years of Pacific bloodshed smouldering deep within living memory, the thought of a remilitarized Japan triggers and inflames recollections that bespeak something akin to treachery. To them, a rebirth of a militarily threatening Japan seems little less than outrageous.

Yet these are residual emotions that tell only part of an evolving story. Today the past is increasingly consigned to historians. The pragmatic demands of an uncertain present now command our attention. Thus, today we find concerned citizens on both sides of the Pacific looking with distinct unease at Japan's current, almost ostrich-like posture toward her own security.

With their respective roles as forces on the international scene now seemingly headed in opposite directions—America downward from the zenith, Japan upward from the nadir—a key question must be asked: Are yesterday's security arrangements for Japan suited to today's realities? It is our good fortune that at this particular point in the history of this vital issue a perceptive political scientist speaks out. Saitama University's Prof. Tetsuya Kataoka has chosen to provide us with an insightful view of where his nation may be headed as it seeks a security posture better suited to tomorrow's international environment. Americans will find the professor's analysis of Japan's motivation in this quest as intriguing as his conclusions. Perhaps most important, we now have a candid exposition of a truly Japanese point of view. What little writing we have hitherto seen on this subject has largely reflected American appraisals.

For years discussion of a credible defense capability had been an untouched and almost untouchable subject in Japanese political dialogue. Then came the mid-1970s. With them came the American exit from Vietnam. In many lands this debacle provided a springboard for changes. Thus, in Japan the time was ripe for gingerly opening public discussion on defense matters. What will result from this discussion? An attempt to answer that question provides the grist for Professor Kataoka's analysis.

Consider the following encapsulation of Kataoka's fascinating thesis. First, he finds Japan now entering an era of national self-reexamination. He then suggests this process may well evolve as follows:

1) Economic growthmanship (his term) will no longer be acceptable as a satisfying national goal in Japan. Some new motivation will be sought to rekindle cohesive national effort.

2) Most likely that new motivation will include a high priority for a *renewed sense of national honor*. In achieving that sense of honor, a self-sufficient national defense capability will become an essential ingredient for Japan.

3) As of now, pacificism is deeply ingrained in the Japanese national psyche. No perception of external threat presently exists of the magnitude needed to prompt Japan to abandon its pacifistic outlook. Accordingly, the motivating force to do so must come from *outside* Japan's borders.

4) This change-inducing external force will likely emerge in the form of some now unknown international crisis—a crisis that will threaten Japan's security. Such a crisis may produce a shock similar to the Pearl Harbor attack that galvanized isolationistic Americans into cohesive global action. Thus, the professor's title—*Waiting for a "Pearl Harbor"*—serves as his descriptive assessment of Japan's present passive but pregnant circumstance.

Kataoka sees the end result of all this to be not only a rearmed Japan, but a change in Japan's democracy. It will be replaced by something he calls "Gaullism." The professor concludes by offering reassurance that this Gaullist republic of tomorrow will be an even "stauncher friend" of the United States than Japan's present democratic state.

Some Americans may feel that elements of Kataoka's thesis are a bit labored. For instance, the suggestion about the need for an external act to force Japan to accept internal change may be questioned. In my view, however, Professor Kataoka makes a useful point here. Abrupt national policy changes in Japan do indeed seem to be triggered by outside events. The Meiji Restoration that followed Admiral Perry's historic visits and Japan's venture into democracy following wartime defeat are the two instances most often cited. In the book *Japanese Society*, Prof. Nakane Chie has noted that the speed with which Japanese policy changes are executed is astonishing once consensus is reached. Outside pressures often help in reaching that consensus.

Changes of even lesser magnitude are also triggered by outside events. During the early 1970s recurrent proposals were made in Japan for procedural reform of the ruling Liberal Democratic Party. Yet it was not until the Lockheed scandal erupted halfway around the world in the 1976 Senate hearings that the Japanese were shocked enough to act. To stipulate the need for a triggering external event to force internal Japanese change is a wholly credible proposition.

The most contentious feature of the author's thesis is, of course, his prediction of an eventual change in the form of the Japanese state. Many Americans who have been delighted with the extent to which postwar Japan has adopted democratic ways may well be horrified to learn that democracy's days may be numbered in that nation. Americans may also be a bit puzzled as to just what will prompt this shift to Gaullism, especially since so many now well-accepted elements mark Japan's political scene. The postwar period has brought to the fore in Japan several effective leaders with a talent for governance of a democracy. Affluence has widened knowledge and travel, enabling the Japanese people to assess democracy in power centers elsewhere in the world. The Imperial institution still stands symbolically and steadily at the center of Japanese society. By outside standards remarkable national pride and unity already exist in Japan. How all of these elements relate to Japan's predicted Gaullist future could well be treated in future writings.

Perhaps as a political scientist, however, Professor Kataoka reaches his conclusion by looking around the world, watching the recent demise of democracy in many lands, and concluding it is no longer suited to the demands of modern national governance. His judgment may also merely reflect aspects of the Japanese scene apparent even to outside observers. Here I have in mind features of traditional Japanese society that seem less than well suited to democratic forms. Among such features are the "vertical" or hierarchical nature of that society and its well-known consensus decision-making process. It must be acknowledged that the society has shown little evident distaste for clusters of economic power such as those modern monoliths, the Japanese trading companies. That such a nation might move toward greater centralization of governmental power should not seem wholly beyond comprehension.

At the same time, however, it must be admitted that contrary impressions are powerfully held by other astute observers. They are convinced that the longer the Japanese practice their postwar democracy the more comfortably do they wear its mantle. Certainly the Japanese people now seem most attracted to such other ideas associated with democracy as an open society and free institutions. The professor's singular thesis of a Gaullist future for Japan will thus no doubt redouble the intensity with which we all watch political developments in that nation in the years ahead.

Perhaps nothing in this paper is more intriguing than the answer the professor provides to the question: Just why will Japan rearm?

His answer: "Not so much to achieve national security as to recapture national honor."

In effect, we are told that in the years ahead the Japanese people will be concerned more with regaining their self-respect than with protecting their shores. Those of us who have for years watched Japan march to an incessant economic drumbeat may be surprised to learn that the nation is about to reverse the focus of its momentum. "Symbolic, rather than material values" will next command Japan's priority attention, says the author. With Japan's historically demonstrated ability to elevate symbolism to high art, no one should dismiss this prospect lightly.

Lest the skeptical be tempted to regard the professor's prediction as unacceptably paradoxical, I suggest we all recall that paradox has been an almost fixed ingredient of the Japanese scene for centuries. Although we may not wish to accept all of the author's surprising conclusions, we must remember that Japan has specialized in producing the improbable.

No doubt Professor Kataoka's wide-ranging experience gave him useful insight into the basis for Japanese policy shifts of the mid-1970s. My diplomatic experience enables me to agree with him that 1975 was indeed a watershed year with respect to the way the Japanese regard their own security. As the U.S. Ambassador in Tokyo during 1974 and early 1975, I was struck by the then subtle, and at times not so subtle, Japanese pressures on the United States. We were repeatedly urged to reduce American military presence in those islands. Then came the American pullout in Southeast Asia. Japan's "go home" pressure on us not only vanished overnight, but it was, in a sense, reversed. The plea to close military bases was replaced by "Do you really need to cut back your forces here?" Within a year Japan's almost complete about-face was evident. In addition to opening public discussion of national security needs, she quickly agreed to establish a mutual defense planning coordination body with the United States. For the first time in a quarter-century the Mutual Security Treaty with the United States did not become a contentious issue in the following national election.

Certainly the pitiful and even pitiable state of Japan's meager self-defense forces made such attention to security matters long overdue. The professor's portrayal of the myriad shortcomings of these forces has the virtue of dramatizing for us the full extent to which Japan's defense policy is still based on U.S. military assistance in the event of an attack anywhere along the shores of that lengthy archipelago. It is indeed fortunate that when Americans are polled today, Japan is the only Asian nation they express willingness to aid in the event of attack.

The gradual shift in perception of her security situation is now enabling Japan to ask herself some serious questions. Perhaps no question is more important than one cited by Professor Kataoka: "In the absence of an adequate defense capability will [Japanese] diplomacy be able to avert any and all military conflicts without presupposing ultimate Finlandization of Japan?

Certainly the Soviets have made it clear they would view a complaisant neighbor across the Japan Sea with great favor. Their huge buildup on the western side of that sea is obviously designed to induce such complaisance.

Americans will find that at times the professor shows a better grasp of Japanese motivations than of American policy intent. This is understandable. Many of us, for instance, will recoil at such contentions as "American officials are so absorbed with the problem of compelling Japan to end the free ride on defense that the thought of having to deal with a nonpacificist Japan never occurs to them."

Most informed Americans would suggest that it is exactly such a thought that has prompted our willingness to continue our security commitments to the Japanese long after they were sufficiently advanced economically and technically to take care of themselves. Given a choice of either a rearmed Japan or a continued American nuclear umbrella, we have shown a clear preference for the umbrella.

With much of the world in ferment as we head into what many are calling the post–Industrial Age, a possible change in the future course of our number-one Asian ally deserves our rapt attention.

Soon after taking office, Japan's Prime Minister Ōhira, aligned himself with those Japanese who seek to bid goodbye to the recent national single-minded concentration on economic progress. Employing a usefully all-en-compassing term, the prime minister tells us that "culture" will be his nation's future focus. In this analysis Professor Kataoka suggests one fallout of this new emphasis on culture, and what it may mean for the Japanese people.

Whether Japan's future course will be that suggested here, the insight into one arc of the spectrum of contemporary Japanese thinking makes this work a valuable contribution. If, as the author suggests, Japan is now "beginning a search for a new definition of greatness," we will all profit by a better understanding of the compulsions that will dictate the direction of that search. Readers will find many of these compulsions well set forth in *Waiting for a "Pearl Harbor."*

JAMES DAY HODGSON

U.S. Ambassador to Japan
1974–1977

Acknowledgments

I wish to thank the following friends for their help in writing this book: Dr. Ramon H. Myers of the Hoover Institution on War, Revolution and Peace, for suggesting the idea of writing it; Prof. Etō Shinkichi of Tokyo University, for reading and criticizing the manuscript; Prof. Chalmers Johnson of the University of California at Berkeley, for his encouragement; Japanese politicians, for having revealed their minds to me; officials of Japan's Defense Agency and the Foreign Ministry (who prefer to be anonymous), for their time; the Defense Agency, for allowing me to reproduce some of the tables and diagrams from its Defense White Paper of 1978; and my wife, Barbara (who, like myself, is a hostage to Japanese-American friendship), for having read, discussed, and typed the manuscript.

The greatest source of inspiration for my undertaking has been George Liska's *Quest for Equilibrium: America and the Balance of Power on Land and Sea* (Baltimore: Johns Hopkins University Press, 1977). Its theoretical rigor and depth of historical insight make it an important statement about world order.

In this book, Japanese names are given surname first, as is the custom. The views offered here are entirely my own.

Introduction

Waiting for a "Pearl Harbor," the title of this book, refers in the first instance to the objective defense posture of the Japanese government; it is implied in the concrete character of the Japanese state as it exists today. I define that character as pacifist commercial democracy and trace its development in chapter one. Japan as a pacifist commercial democracy cannot take care of her legitimate national defense needs until a security crisis knocks on the door. Assuming that the Japanese people would resolve to defend themselves in such a crisis, they would have a double crisis to deal with, for they would have to change the character of their state before they could cope with a security crisis.

Japan's defense posture is a reflection of the nature of the regime, or the political system. It is the official policy of Japan to maintain a bare minimum of military capability in peacetime, but to mobilize all national resources to cope with a crisis larger than could be handled by the force in being. In other words, Japan's Self-Defense Forces (SDFs), together with armed forces of the United States, are expected to function as a screen behind which the country will mobilize in the event of a serious threat to her security. It is my judgment that the SDFs as presently organized cannot serve that purpose.

Will Japan then collapse in the face of a threat? That possibility cannot be ruled out, so deep is pacifist sentiment nurtured by the Japanese state. But it would be safer to assume that Japan will somehow survive the crisis and go on. That is only half the problem, however. For in surviving a future security crisis, she will have survived a political crisis as well: she will have turned from pacifist commercial democracy to something else. Nobody is giving thought to this problem. So absorbed are American officials with the current problem of compelling Japan to end the free ride on American defense that the thought of having to deal with a nonpacifist Japan never occurs to them.

A nation maintains an army to keep the peace. And yet a security crisis cannot always be avoided. If in a crisis Japan must transform the character of the state—and her defense posture promises nothing less than that—then should we not be *Waiting for a "Pearl Harbor"*? Should we not anticipate this change in the Japanese regime and come to some agreement on it? This is the second meaning of the title.

The United States had a hand in founding the Japanese regime; yet today the American people find it defective and wanting—as, indeed, do many Japanese. The reason is obvious: depending on America for matters of life and death has bred a psychology that takes America's indulgence for granted. If therefore a change in the Japanese regime is unavoidable, we had better be ready to improve on it.

In my estimate, the most likely form the Japanese state will take on the morrow of a security crisis is Gaullism: Japan will be fully capitalist, but more republican than democratic in character; she will be a true equal of the United States in a defensive alliance and an even stauncher friend than today; but she will ask for autonomy in defense of the western Pacific. A recent shift in Japan's public opinion points in the Gaullist direction. This is also the most logical solution to the problems of the Japan-U.S. alliance, which have been festering since America's retreat from Vietnam.

CHAPTER ONE

Rousing from Slumber?

Reversing a tradition of more than thirty years, Japan began in 1978 to debate in earnest questions of military defense. The tradition had been to frame defense questions as sterile constitutional issues, and to ask whether a given level of armament is permitted. This time the Japanese are debating how much and what kind of arms are necessary; they are debating defense questions on their own terms. "Earnest" would be the best adjective to describe the debate: though there are few shrill voices and no hysteria, it is extensive and will continue regardless of who is in power. The man who was instrumental in triggering the debate was Prime Minister Fukuda Takeo. Fukuda must be credited with masterful timing; but then, the ground was long ready. A shift in Japanese outlook and consciousness had become perceptible toward the end of the war in Vietnam, and it gradually acquired momentum. The defense debate issues from that consciousness. It is murky, for it springs from the deep recesses of the Japanese mind, which this brooding nation seldom reveals to outsiders. That consciousness, in a word, is nationalism.

A few examples illustrate a facet of the new consciousness. The weekly magazine *Asahi Journal*, which is devoted to news reporting and commentaries, has an extensive and well-educated audience—somewhat to the left of center—who would likely describe themselves as conscientious intellectuals. Spiro Agnew might well have called them effete intellectual snobs. The magazine has been the citadel of pacifism, of opposition to constitutional amendment, and of ideas like unarmed neutrality. Its first issue in 1979 was devoted to the topic "Dreams of Nippon as a great power." Since shortly after publication of Herman Kahn's *The Emerging Japanese Superstate* in 1971, which sold well in Japan, a consensus has obtained that Japan is an economic power (*keizai taikoku*) with corresponding "responsibilities." But *Asahi Journal's* special issue was about Japan not as an economic power, but simply as a

power or a great power. I was as startled by it as if I had picked up a copy of
Partisan Review and found *National Review* between the covers instead.

Another example: an animated cartoon movie has been playing to a
standing-room-only crowd of teenagers for weeks on end. Its remarkable
popularity has turned it into an object of scrutiny by commentators and
pundits. The film has to do with a fictitious saga of *Yamato*, the biggest
battleship in the world, built by the Imperial Navy. Shorn of air cover toward
the end of the Pacific War, the Imperial Navy faced this choice with respect to
Yamato. It could idle at anchor waiting to be sunk by the U.S. Navy, or it could
go on a doomed mission with its guns blazing, merely to keep the Imperial
Navy's honor clean. In the end the second course was chosen. So the mighty
Yamato put to sea on its last mission and was duly sunk. This is where the
movie begins, and it goes on to depict the miraculous resurrection of the
battleship from the bottom of the sea. *Yamato* is refurbished and refitted to
become a spaceship, and it goes into outer space to do battle with forces of
evil that threaten our planet. At the start of the film the audience is treated to
the scene of *Yamato* gliding majestically out of the Inland Sea to the tune of
the "Battleship March," the "Anchors Aweigh" of the Imperial Navy. A
fisherman and his little son wave *Yamato* on from a dinghy. And the old man
says to his boy, "Look, that's the ship that belongs to us, Japanese men."

Again, the point may be lost to those unfamiliar with the state of Japanese
public opinion throughout the postwar years: it would have been unthink-
able ten years ago to present the doomed combat and lost war with anything
but utter cynicism, let alone to find glory in death. To be sure, there has been
a minority of dissenters, but they could not get a public hearing. But the tide
has started to turn, and Japanese public opinion is churning.

During the Lincoln-Douglas debate, Abraham Lincoln was moved to say,
"In a country such as ours public opinion is everything." Today Japan, too, is
a democracy in a decisive sense. If ever Japan were to change her basic
orientation—and the defense question touches on her constitution—it would
not be because a handful of men swap places at the top, as has happened
lately in China. Rather, it would be through a protracted and arduous process
of gestation and consensus formation involving many detours, stops, and
starts. The closest analogue in American history to what is happening in
Japan today would be the debate between the America Firsters and the
Internationalists on the eve of Pearl Harbor. (Japan has even produced a Billy
Mitchell of her own!) The process of policy formation in Japan is befuddling
even to experienced observers. It is all the more important, then, for the

United States not to take its bearing by surface phenomena but to grasp, insofar as possible, the fundamental forces that are agitating Japan and the direction in which she may be heading.

The defense question in Japan ultimately leads to the question of autonomy in national defense. But Article IX of the Peace Constitution forbids Japan to possess any but the minimum capabilities necessary for self-defense. Many an American has wondered aloud, "Why not repeal Article IX? We are working on the twenty-seventh amendment to our constitution." But the comparison is misleading. Article IX is not, say, a prohibition amendment that can be added and removed as public taste changes. Article IX is to the Japanese constitution what the right to life, liberty, and the pursuit of happiness is to the American constitution: more than mere written words on a piece of document, it has become the very essence of the Japanese regime or polity. In other words, in and around the Peace Constitution imposed by the Supreme Commander for the Allied Powers (SCAP), Japanese society has grown and articulated itself. This regime can be defined as pacifist commercial democracy. It is very stable and prosperous, a good friend of America, but dependent on the United States for external security. Yet, questions of national defense do of necessity touch on a nation's autonomy and sovereignty, and in that sense they pose this question in turn: Should the pacifist commercial democratic regime in Japan be broken up and replaced by a new arrangement? Nationalistic opinion, mentioned above, is raising precisely this question.

One somewhat schematic way of visualizing the various constitutional interpretations and corresponding defense postures is to think of Japan as in tension between three basic forces. The first, on the left of the political spectrum and fast shrinking, is opposed to possession of any arms and rests its case on a certain reading of the constitution. The second, to the right of the first, is the mainstream of the Japanese polity and is anchored in the solid majority of people. It agrees to the need for a minimum capability for self-defense but generally views Japan's self-help as a supplement to the protection provided by the United States. Thus it supports the Japan-U.S. Security Treaty* and is prepared to live with Japan's unequal status vis-à-vis the United States. This group, too, rests its case on the constitution; that is, on a different reading of it. Conceivably, the second group, which is basically

---

*Treaty of Mutual Cooperation and Security between Japan and the United States, signed at Washington, D.C., on January 19, 1960.

pacifist in outlook as judged by any standard applicable in the world today, could be persuaded to accept a larger burden of defense and an autonomous defense posture if, for instance, the alliance with the United States falls apart.

The third group, opposed to the above two, wants to provide for greater autonomy in national defense. Naturally, it is on the right of its pacifist opponents; but opposition to pacifism does not necessarily make one a right-winger—in other countries most men in this third group would find themselves among the conservatives to the right of center. This group wants to amend Article IX at minimum; it is in favor of continuing the alliance with the United States but on more equal terms. The group is small, top-heavy, and wields influence out of proportion to its size because it includes senior Liberal-Democratic party (LDP) politicians, some big businessmen, and opinion leaders. In my judgment Fukuda Takeo, Kishi Nobusuke (both former prime ministers), and Nakasone Yasuhiro, former minister of the Defense Agency, are in this group. They are Gaullist in outlook.

Not everyone in the third group raises the constitutional issue—for the time being. Rather, they carry on their debate on relative terms, such as the number of divisions or the share of the gross national product (GNP) to be devoted to arms expenditure. On the surface, therefore, the debate between the second and third groups seems to be about "more" or "less." But what motivates the third group is not merely concern about security; in addition it is interested in the question of the nation's honor and status. Hence the real underlying issue in Japan's defense debate is security versus security plus honor.

FOUNDING THE PACIFIST STATE

The defense controversy will increasingly turn on the adequacy of the pacifist commercial democracy to provide for Japan's security and enable her to play an honorable role internationally; a brief review of the origin and development of that regime is therefore in order. The review will show how, in spite of recurrent challenges, the Peace Constitution struck roots in the Japanese soil and grew into the existing regime. That regime had its origin in overwhelming defeat in a total war. The United States, too, has tasted of defeat in war in the recent past, and the American people are now in a unique, though not pleasant, position to appreciate and empathize with the depth of Japan's pacifism. Such appreciation is preliminary to coming to some conclusions on whether Japan is enjoying a free ride under American protection.

There are four landmark events in the career of the pacifist commercial democratic regime: 1) Japan's defeat in war and the imposition of the Peace Constitution; 2) the Korean War, which compelled the United States to offer a unilateral guarantee for Japan's defense; 3) the anti–Security Treaty struggle of 1960, an ersatz civil war that reaffirmed the legitimacy of the Peace Constitution; and 4) the defeat of Japan's former conqueror in Vietnam.

War is a catharsis of history. It reduces to simple, black and white answers complex and baffling questions that an army of historians might never solve to their mutual satisfaction. All the more so if the conflict is intense and ideological, as was the war in the Pacific. Even in Vietnam, a much smaller conflict, it was possible to argue the pros and cons with plausibility until the end came in defeat for the United States. At that point, everyone submits to the verdict passed on the battlefield: a lost war can never be a "good war." Perhaps this is the true meaning of that seemingly abominable remark by Gen. Douglas MacArthur, "There is no substitute for victory." For the vanquished almost certainly feel that they have been simply in the wrong, and they do so without external compulsion. Would there be American youths waving the Vietcong flag on every college campus had the fortunes of the United States been different?

Knowing today the toll exacted by her own lost war, the United States can understand the extent of derangement in Japanese psyche since 1945. But America's defeat in Vietnam was so slight and indirect as to defy comparison with Japan's. The government of Hanoi did not send an expeditionary force to bring the United States to heel; it even permitted the United States to extricate itself from the war "with honor." It merely refused to grant a decent interval between that and the fall of Saigon.

Nevertheless, the impact of a lost war is identical in nature everywhere. Denigrating a particular state that sustained defeat, it denigrates the country itself. Localism becomes preferable to nationalism or internationalism. People turn away from public affairs and scurry to the comfort of private lives. The public realm almost disappears, for there is much in the being of the state that depends on myth, and the right or authority of the state cannot be adduced rationally from the sum of individual interests. In interstate relations, a defeated state almost certainly becomes a nonentity; it will not recover its political will and assertiveness for a long time. On the other hand, economic activity, in the original Greek sense of managing the affairs of a household, is perfectly compatible with a nation politically castrated in total defeat—witness Japan's phenomenal success in the postwar years. The talk of "interdependence," that is, economic interdependence, in post-Vietnam Washington can be regarded as another species that belongs to the same genus.

Defeat also erases the distinction between "just wars" and "unjust wars," or between legitimate self-defense and acts of aggression; all wars are bad in a society afflicted with deepest cynicism. Deserters and turncoats become heroes, whereas the heroes of yesteryear are now villains. Indeed, there is a kind of "transvaluation of values" as the society goes topsy-turvy. And why not, when the emperor himself is shown to be without clothes? In short, there is nothing that makes the state look shabbier, more degraded, and less legitimate than losing a war. It was under circumstances like these that the new Japanese state had to be founded.

The sense of remorse, guilt, shame, penitence, and withdrawal that afflicted the Japanese upon defeat in World War II was amplified by the Far Eastern Military Tribunal's proceedings and by many occupation reforms. When the question of a war crimes trial arose, the British government had doubts about its wisdom. The British apparently felt the idea was quixotic, and they proposed instead simple execution of Japanese leaders. In retrospect, that seemingly barbaric idea was not so barbaric. A nation of samurai might have understood it as the natural way of warfare. (In fact, that is how the trial is accepted today.) But simple execution of Japanese leaders did not suit the legal-moralistic inclination of America: convinced that she had just won the war to end all wars, the United States demanded nothing less than punishment for Japan's "crime against humanity" as a precondition for remaking the nature of the Japanese.

America's vision for the postwar world was Wilsonian in some respects and revisionist in others. Franklin Roosevelt, the architect of that vision, shared with Woodrow Wilson the assumption that the last war was behind him, and that the League of Nations should be resurrected as the governing organ for the postwar world. But the United Nations, the League's successor, was not to be merely a parliamentary assembly of sovereign states; it was to have a political will based on the consensus and cooperation of the "four policemen" sitting in the Security Council. The unrevised Wilsonianism was represented by the Bretton Woods Agreement and a host of other international economic agreements. The organs created by these agreements were entrusted with the task of building a world economic order that would be stable, access-free, and equitable in distributing the benefits of the free enterprise system. Japan was to be gradually refitted into the new world order—after proper punishment and purge of those who had had a part in the imperialist scheme.

The task of reforming Japan as the precondition for that reintegration fell mostly to Douglas MacArthur and his staff, packed full of New Deal idealists, who launched themselves posthaste on the democratizing mission. But recent researches into the occupation period reveal that this democratization was a means, not an end in itself. The singularly overriding goal of U.S. occupation policy was to prevent the recurrence of imperialist aggression by seeing to it that Japan was disarmed. Indeed, the lesson of Nazi Germany rising out of the peace of Versailles was fresh on the minds of Allied leaders; and preventing revanchism among the perpetrators of Pearl Harbor became the supreme desideratum of occupation policy.

The economic policies of Roosevelt's new world order turned out to be a phenomenal success, but his political assumption, having to do with the United Nations as world government, shortly proved itself false. The world refused to transform itself into a mass of quietly grazing sheep watched over by four policemen. Interstate relations remained very much political. Only in Japan among the major countries of the world does one find the absence of political will combined with the best application to the Bretton Woods system. I submit that it is a measure of the success of American occupation policy that this is so.

Many occupation-instituted reforms were designed specifically to insure Japan's peaceableness. Her entire educational system was changed; and SCAP supervised the writing of new textbooks to instill the idea that, to use a MacArthur phrase, Japan should become the "Switzerland of Asia." Judo was banned because it was considered a martial art. Wartime leaders who had escaped trial were purged from public office. The media were under tight censorship. These and a myriad of other measures buttressed and reinforced the verdict of the Far Eastern Military Tribunal. It was the time of "one hundred million in penitence together," as one prime minister would put it.

It did not occur to ordinary Japanese to suspect that one-sidedness and immaturity might be implied in that verdict. This realization came much later, when they witnessed the United States fighting a war much like their own in the very country that they had earlier surrendered. In the meantime, the Japanese did not question the verdict because, for one thing, the conquerors, fresh on the heels of their exhilarating victory, thought of themselves as above reproach. As Daniel Bell of Harvard would write shortly thereafter: ideology having ended in America, she knew only the truth.

At this point the origin of Article IX of the new constitution—an article still very much alive and binding—must be touched upon briefly. It must be apparent from the foregoing that under no circumstances could Japan be allowed to retain the means of waging war. But a constitutional ban was not the most obvious means of keeping Japan disarmed. A four-power treaty between the United States, the Soviet Union, Britain, and China to keep a tight leash on Japan was considered; but in fact the idea of a self-imposed constitutional ban pre-empted this choice.

The thought of a disarmed Japan relying mostly on U.N. collective security, once hailed as a brave new idea, has since fallen in disrepute in many quarters; during the Eisenhower administration, Richard Nixon even condemned it as a mistake. Then the question of who first proposed it became a kind of family squabble between Americans and Japanese, each blaming the other for the initiative. Douglas MacArthur, who was entrusted with the plenary power to write the new constitution, has given us to understand retrospectively that Prime Minister Shidehara came up with the idea in a moment of contrition. Obviously this is a technical question, inasmuch as disarmament was unavoidable. Still, it is not only an interesting point to speculate on but also quite germane to U.S.-Japanese friendship. And speculation is all that is possible, for there is no clinching evidence extant from the meeting of MacArthur and Shidehara on January 24, 1946, at which they settled on Article IX. As reconstructed masterfully by Japanese historian Hata Ikuhiko, the following is what transpired.[1]

The Potsdam Declaration, which laid down the terms of Japan's surrender, left the question of the emperor's status deliberately open; but the threat of continued atomic bombardment forced Tokyo to accept the declaration. When MacArthur and Shidehara met, the Far Eastern Military Tribunal had just started, and the attitude in Allied capitals was quite hostile to the idea of sparing the emperor from the trial. His fate hung in the balance. But MacArthur was convinced that the success of the occupation rested on the immunity of the emperor, as well as the emperor system itself, and that their violation would lead to revanchism in Japan. Shidehara was of the same mind, of course. At the January 24 meeting, according to Hata, Shidehara proposed what amounted to swapping the safety of the emperor for a constitutional ban on armament. He calculated that the idea of a constitutional ban would take the sting off the impact of the news that the emperor would remain on the throne. Would not Japan with the emperor be nevertheless tame if she were disarmed forever? Shidehara calculated correctly.

Article IX states that "the Japanese forever renounce war as a sovereign right of the nation." Yet today Japan's SDFs, with a total of 240,000 men and women in uniform, rank seventh in the world in terms of defense expenditure. How is this possible? The stock-in-trade answer of the Japanese left is that Japanese "reactionaries," in league with American "cold warriors," most notably John Foster Dulles, have twisted the constitution out of shape. But this is not so, at least not formally. In the process of drafting the constitution, the parliamentary committee under Ashida Hitoshi with the consent of SCAP deliberately phrased the article so that, although Japan is indeed forbidden to possess "land, sea, and air forces" as a "means of settling international disputes," she is not thereby deprived of the inherent right of self-defense. What sort of arms constitute the means of settling international disputes, and what sort constitute the means of self-defense, is vague and relative. But it would be a serious mistake for anyone to assume that the ban in Article IX is wholly relative or that it means virtually nothing. It does impose an upper ceiling in arms acquisition, it dictates Japan's strategy, and, most important, it shapes the character of the Japanese polity.

Precisely because Article IX does mean something, it poses a grave implication for Japan's future. The article seems to ordain that any future crisis involving a threat to Japan's security will be a constitutional crisis as well. The defense posture permissible under the constitution is far from adequate, even for the stated purpose of self-defense. Nevertheless, if Japan resolves to defend herself in a crisis, as I hope she will, she will have to amend the constitution first. As will be noted below, Japan's defense planners are painfully aware of this constitutional straightjacket and have put together a defense posture that is in close parallel to it. Together these constitute the posture of "waiting for a Pearl Harbor." As I use the phrase here, it means two things. Objectively it means the postponement of important decisions until a crisis occurs. Subjectively it means that some men with the perspicacity to perceive the implications of the posture may be waiting for a crisis in order to have their way. The self-styled friends of "democracy" in Japan seem to be oblivious of this fact, and they continue to oppose constitutional amendment in peacetime.

THE KOREAN WAR

Much to the consternation of General MacArthur and his staff, within no more than half a year of the promulgation of the constitution in November 1946, pressure to rearm Japan and to scuttle some of the New Deal-like reforms began to emanate from Washington. Relations between the United States and the Soviet Union were deteriorating. But so abrupt a reversal of key occupation policies, MacArthur feared, would lead to American (and to his own) loss of prestige in the eyes of the Japanese. It was from about 1947 on that the phrase "the Switzerland of Asia" began to appear in his thoughts. The proconsul stood between Tokyo and Washington to cushion the latter's pressure on Japan to rearm. Not even the outbreak of war in Korea could cause him to abandon his constitution. Without his intervention Japan might well have succumbed to the whimsical swing of the pendulum in Washington. But if Japan were to preserve her constitution intact and remain unarmed, some means had to be found to insure her external safety. That search was hastened because of MacArthur's desire to end the occupation before it alienated the Japanese.

To insure Japan's security there were several alternatives, depending on the state of U.S.-Soviet relations. First was the guarantee of Japan's unarmed neutrality by the United States, the Soviet Union, Britain, and China. A second was Japan's rapid remilitarization to the point where she could look after her own security against minor challenges. A third was the U.S. guarantee of Japan's security. A four-power guarantee would have been compatible in principle both with continued wartime Allied cooperation and with the cold war. The second and third alternatives presupposed a breakdown in wartime Allied cooperation, and Japan's drawing closer to the United States and away from the Soviet Union. Interestingly, it was the Socialist government, the only one in all of postwar history, that opted for the last alternative. In a memorandum designed to elicit American response, Foreign Minister Ashida Hitoshi of the Katayama cabinet proposed this scheme: Japan would accept the continued U.S. military presence in Okinawa with an option to use bases in the Japanese home islands in an emergency. In return for these basing rights, the United States would promise to protect Japan against external threat from the Soviet Union. (China was still undergoing civil strife at this stage.) This is the essence of the Japan-U.S. Security Treaty, which has been supported to date by conservative parties. It fell to Yoshida Shigeru, a prewar liberal and an astute diplomat who organized the conservative government that succeeded the Socialists, to implement this scheme through the peace negotiations that followed in 1950–51.

Yoshida saw a boon to Japan in the emerging cold war. He did not fabricate the cold war, nor can he justly be blamed for having exploited it. But a boon it was nonetheless; for in its absence Japan would have been destined to submit to a punitive occupation, reparation, and indefinite surveillance by the Allied powers. Instead, as the Iron Curtain descended along the lines of American and Soviet occupation, Japan and West Germany came to be looked upon in Washington as assets to be guarded against Soviet encroachment. These vanquished foes turned into America's friends in the cold war—so much so that after the Chinese intervention in the Korean War, some Americans began to wonder whether they had fought the wrong enemies in World War II.

Yoshida had been in active diplomatic service before the war, when China had slowly displaced Japan as America's friend in Asia, and he saw in the cold war a chance to restore the old relationship and to go on to forge a defensive alliance between Japan and the United States.

He wanted an alliance, not a unilateral guarantee that would turn Japan into a dependency. But his objective was inherently contradictory to another he pursued: to keep Japan free of the burden of heavy armament. Japan, then completely in ruins, existed hand-to-mouth at the American taxpayers' expense. Too, the defeat and the liberalizing occupation reforms had given rise to a strong pacifist sentiment supported by the Japan Socialist party (JSP), the Communists, and the labor movement, and it would have been very imprudent to pose a divisive issue to the fragile body politic.

With MacArthur's strong endorsement, Yoshida set for Japan the task of economic recovery and the maintenance of a low political posture. He envisioned Japan as a commercial democracy that draws her sustenance and vitality from integration in the Wilsonian world of free enterprise centered in North America. His counsel to his followers in the conservative party can be characterized as dialectical: the weaker and the more debilitated Japan was, the more she would have to draw close to Imperial America for protection. In time, as Japan regained strength, she could also regain autonomy.

Soon Yoshida was accused by conservative critics of subservience to the United States. Whether aware of it or not, he was steering Japan in the direction of pacifist commercial democracy. His disciples, who took his counsel to heart, included such successful prime ministers as Ikeda Hayato, Satō Eisaku, and Ōhira Masayoshi.

John Foster Dulles, Yoshida's opposite number in negotiating the peace treaty, saw the contradiction in his position and hammered away at it. Dulles brushed aside Yoshida's plea for a semblance of equality: an alliance. That, he said, was possible only between equals who contributed mutually to the security of both. He insisted that Japan conform to the demand of the Vandenberg Resolution, which translated into "self-help" with a 350,000-man army capable of repulsing Soviet invasion. In addition, he insisted that Japan commit herself to the regional security of the entire Far East; having driven Japan out of Taiwan and Korea, he was demanding status quo ante, as it were. Yoshida would countenance only an expanded constabulary force for internal security functions, and he refused any role for Japan in regional security. His only quid pro quo was the offer of base rights in Japan, which amounted to an invitation for continued U.S. occupation, a point his domestic critics were quick to notice.

Dulles's attempt to undo the "MacArthur constitution" was unsuccessful, and the negotiation deadlocked. But the outbreak of the Korean War in June 1950 overtook him. President Truman's decision to hold on to the Korean buffer made sense only as a means of defending Japan. A de facto guarantee of Japan's security was in effect. The original Security Treaty, signed simultaneously with the Peace Treaty in San Francisco in 1951, was a reflection of this state of affairs. But the only concrete contract in it had to do with the right of the United States to station her troops in Japan and to use Japan as a staging area for operations in the Far East. There was no American guarantee, de jure, to defend Japan; the treaty was unequal, as Yoshida's conservative critics noted.[2]

In this way, the Peace Constitution acquired a safeguard against external threat. It is worth remembering that Korea was the hinge that connected pacifist Japan with the United States. When President Carter announced the withdrawal of ground combat units from Korea in 1977, defense consciousness heightened visibly in Japan.

CRITICS OF THE ALLIANCE

With great temerity, and with apologies for many exceptions, one can define the alignment of postwar Japanese politics in terms of three groups. 1) The radical-liberals (*kakushin*) on the left consisted of the Communists, the Socialists of the left (especially when their party was split), and the "conscientious intellectuals" of neo-Marxist persuasion who dominated the media. 2) Slightly to the right of center were mainstream conservatives, organized into the Liberal-Democratic party in 1955 and led by the disciples of the Yoshida School, so-called, recruited from elite government bureaucracies.* 3) To the right of them but within the LDP were professional politicians with considerable prewar experience. The left and the right turned into critics of Yoshida's and his successors' stewardship of the alliance. Both their cases rested formally on the desirability of greater autonomy from the United States.

---

*In Japan, as in France, the highest achievers from the best universities enter the civil service because it carries the highest social prestige. It is as though all the law clerks from the Harvard and Yale law schools went into public administration.

The radical-liberals were the first to make known their opposition to the peace and security treaties package. Whereas Yoshida reasoned that the constitutional ban on war left Japan no recourse but to rely on the United States for protection, the radical-liberals started from the same premise and argued for "unarmed neutrality." In one sense the radical-liberals were part of the worldwide movement of neutralism generated by the tensions of extreme bipolarization. They maintained the argument, later conceded by their counterpart in America, the counterculture, that the cold war had arisen due to Washington's provocation and initiative. It was not Japan's war, and she would gratuitously antagonize China and the Soviet Union by entangling herself in an alliance with America. They opposed the "partial peace" at San Francisco and demanded "all-round peace" with all former belligerents, including China and the Soviet Union.

The ideological anti-Americanism of the radical-liberals was of a piece with the doctrinaire Marxism of the left-wing Socialists and the neo-Marxism of the so-called conscientious intellectuals. At the same time, Imperial America at the height of the cold war crusade tended to ride roughshod over the lately vanquished former foe and thus strengthened the hands of the radical-liberals. According to the Security Treaty, Japan was under an obligation to provide its bases for whatever operation the United States chose to undertake in Asia; Japan was in danger of being willy-nilly involved in wars not of her own choosing. In fact, John Foster Dulles twisted Yoshida's arm into supporting the Chinese Nationalists in Taiwan against the mainland by making that a condition for peace at San Francisco. In the end, the radical-liberals exposed themselves as negative oppositionists, but while the U.S. presence in Asia (for example, in the form of army bases) was dominant they had a lease on life.

The cold war in Asia was directed mainly against China and those who were thought to be her proxies, and this boded ill for Yoshida and the conservatives. The opposition had had a genuine fear of Russia, but when it came to Mao's China it had no fear at all. It was as if the pan-Asianism of the prewar right wing had transferred itself to the postwar left while the pro-Anglo-Americanism of the prewar center-left had shifted to the postwar conservatives. This state of affairs continued until the Nixon shock—Nixon's going to Peking with no prior notice and adding a 10-percent surcharge on Japan's exports to the United States—rekindled pan-Asian sentiment among the right.

The protests by the left were in a sense a form of pacifist withdrawal and self-denial and would have counted for less but for this fact: the protesters found in Article IX of the constitution a rallying point for action. They believed they had found in the constitution the only avenue for exercising autonomy from "American imperialism." But a convoluted psychology lay behind this.

The radical-liberals and "conscientious intellectuals" suffered from deep-seated guilt at what Japan had wrought in Asia—and, in fact, at what Japan had been since as far back as the beginning of her modernization in the nineteenth century. They subscribed to Herbert Norman's history of modern Japan, the Bible of the New Dealers at SCAP headquarters. Norman argued that modern Japan was in fact a carry-over of feudalism from the Middle Ages; Japan's sickness, which reached to the very core, had existed from time immemorial. In this they were precursors of those American intellectuals of the counterculture whose revisionism did not end with Vietnam but reached all the way back to the opening of the American West, the Indian wars, and the Spanish-American War. Japan's radical-liberals were no less self-flagellant; they seemed to take to heart the assumption of the Far Eastern Military Tribunal that the only depravity in the world existed among the Japanese, and that all that was necessary to create a peaceful world was for them to repent, reform, and withdraw.

Their anti-Americanism, one surmises, was derivative of their sense of guilt. The point is illustrated in the following passage written by Shimizu Ikutarō, a well-known Tokyo University professor (as so many "conscientious intellectuals" were) and the leading spokesman of the anti–Security Treaty struggle of 1960:

> Along with the rise of victim-consciousness, the bitter offender-consciousness of postwar days seems to have gradually dissipated. If I may simplify the matter to the extreme, our autonomy resting on the dark regrets of having been the offender and barely propped up by the constitution has receded, and the consciousness of being a passive victim has surfaced. And the dissipation of the offender-consciousness means precisely that the China question is disappearing from Japanese consciousness.[3]

Shimizu is counseling his countrymen against protesting Hiroshima, exhorting them instead to repent their crimes—especially in China. As an act of penitence and expurgation, he wants them to live up to the ideals of the Peace constitution. That the constitution was handed down by the Americans made it even sweeter, perhaps, for it gave him the wherewithal not only to chastise himself but to chastise America with a vengeance. He feels betrayed not by the America that punished Japan with hellfire, but by the America that gave him the Peace Constitution only to desert him and go on to repeat Japan's crime in Asia. Here is the makeup of the Japanese pacifist: defender of the verdict of the Tokyo Trial, anti-American, and in the mainstream until Saigon fell.

CHALLENGE FROM THE RIGHT

Japan's leading conservative politicians in the immediate postwar years—divided among several shifting parties—were carry-overs from the prewar years. A substantial number of them were driven from public offices by the SCAP-instituted purge, and a few were even incarcerated as war criminals. Power fell to men, like Yoshida, who had a record of altercation with the prewar military establishment and were therefore "clean."

Yoshida had another strength: he hailed from the Foreign Ministry. The occupation of Japan, unlike that of West Germany, was indirect, with SCAP administering the country through indigenous government bureaucracies. If any of Japan's prewar ruling organs survived occupation reforms more or less intact, one was the civil service system. When the purge left a gaping hole among the ranks of conservative politicians, Yoshida came up with an innovation that was later institutionalized: he recruited elite bureaucrats from central ministries into politics. Many leading bureaucrat-politicians owe their beginnings to Yoshida's patronage, and to date they constitute a rather ill-defined group that goes by the name of "mainstream," graduates of the "Yoshida School." Though highly nebulous, the sociological correlation between elite bureaucrats and pro-American conservative politics has some marginal significance.

Returning to public life when the purge was lifted at the end of the occupation, the old party professionals were disgruntled by what they saw as Yoshida's power grab. Partisan resentment of Yoshida, who served as prime minister for eight years, was superimposed upon their dislike of his American patron, with whom he had a close working relationship. They suspected that Yoshida used SCAP to purge his political enemies. The professionals decided to unseat him in what was to become the first challenge by the right against the pacifist commerical democratic regime.

It was natural that modification of foreign-inspired reforms was inevitable if only for the sake of consolidating them. Nevertheless, it is interesting to speculate whether the movement for constitutional revision and its recurrence in 1960 could have turned into a clear-cut challenge to the regime. In the end, the first challenge fizzled out; the second one touched off an ersatz civil war and ended up reaffirming the regime at a higher level. One obvious constraint against the revolt by the right was the pacifist sentiment that suffused society. Another was the anti-communism, especially the strong aversion to Communist China, among the politicians on the right—which forfeited for them an alternative to the American ally. It must be noted that both these constraints are much weaker today—an important fact because the leaders of both the first and second challenges were incipiently Gaullist, committed to American values but detached from the United States.

What motivated Yoshida's opponents, led by Hatoyama Ichirō, was nationalism and a desire to restore the primacy of politics over economism and bureaucratism. They professed to believe that Yoshida's close liaison with SCAP and Washington was "subservience"; and as an indispensable precondition for regaining autonomy, they proposed amending Article IX. "The present constitution," said Hatoyama, "was imposed on us in English when neither the government nor the people had had freedom. It must take a very patient man to be grateful to it. It was drawn up with a view to sapping our strength."[4] Rearmament of Japan would also rid her of U.S. armed forces stationed there. But along with the amendment, Hatoyama wanted to carry out many reforms (for example, recentralization of the police administration and stronger anti-labor measures) that would undo what he considered excesses of the occupation. To end Japan's "subservience" to the United States, he was interested in reopening peace negotiations with the Soviet Union.

It is not as easy to assess Hatoyama's achievement as is commonly thought. A pedestrian view holds that he accomplished little: normalization of a Japanese-Soviet relationship that fell short of a full-fledged peace treaty including territorial settlement. This view seems to reflect Yoshida's derisive comment that Japan was "not strong enough" to be autonomous. The failure of Hatoyama's incipient Gaullism was a warning to those who would propose to rewrite the constitution and readjust the Japanese-U.S. relationship without being very clear-minded about all the ramifications or alternatives. But Hatoyama must be credited with one change that has had an enormous potential impact. In 1955 the Socialists—who were split in 1951 over the question of "partial" versus "all-round peace"—came together. This in turn prompted the splintered conservatives to unite into the LDP. Hatoyama was chiefly instrumental in writing into the LDP party program the objectives of constitutional revision and rearmament.

But constitutional revision was effectively blocked by the fact that the Socialists and the Communists together controlled more than one-third of

the parliamentary seats. Hatoyama tried to reduce the opposition by changing the electoral laws, without success. The LDP resigned itself for the time
being to the status quo. But there was one man who was determined to
implement the LDP party program, and his confrontation with the radical-
liberals over revision of the original Security Treaty constitutes the third
phase in the career of the pacifist commercial democratic regime. In my
judgment, that confrontation was to the Peace Constitution what the American Civil War was to the constitution of the Union: when the forces seeking
revision were defeated, the spirit of the founders was reaffirmed.

Kishi Nobusuke, who succeeded Hatoyama as prime minister in 1957, was
an enigmatic man even among Japan's usually silent conservative politicians.
A close friend of Tōjō Hideki's, he served in the wartime government and
was imprisoned as a war criminal before returning to politics. His forte was
economic planning, in the forerunner of today's MITI (Ministry of
International Trade and Industry). Some of his early ideas showed a strong
inclination toward priority for the public interest over private property. He
was highly critical of the spirit of dependence that permeated Japan, and he
held that relying on the United States for matters of life and death was the
crux of Japan's problem. In particular, he was resolved to revise the Security
Treaty of 1951—whereby the United States guaranteed Japan's security unilaterally—toward greater "mutuality."

It is common to ascribe much of the tension generated during the ensuing
crisis of 1960 to Kishi's high-handed style, his "reactionary" background,
and his handling of the passage of the revised treaty through the parliament.
Indeed, he lacked finesse and prudence in parliamentary tactics. But I disagree with the thesis that, had Kishi not been in charge, a revised and more
"mutual" treaty would have passed without a hitch. The Security Treaty was
only ostensibly the issue. Any revision of the 1951 treaty toward greater
mutuality would have meant greater sharing by Japan in her own defense and
ultimately even in the defense of the United States. The issue was the
constitution, and Kishi was challenging the pacifist commercial regime itself.[5]

The mobilization of four million demonstrators against the Kishi government indicated that the opposition understood wherein the issue lay. President Eisenhower's goodwill trip to Japan was canceled, and Kishi seriously
contemplated calling the troops of the SDFs to quell the riots. After ramming
the new Security Treaty—still unequal—through the parliament, Kishi resigned.

CHAPTER TWO

The Victory of Growthmanship

For managing to pass the new Security Treaty, and for holding on to power after the fall of the Kishi cabinet, the LDP congratulated itself. But its victory was very questionable, for there was a high price attached. That became apparent when Ikeda Hayato, Kishi's successor, resolved that all major political issues that might arouse the opposition would have to be avoided if the LDP were to stay in power. Upon careful deliberation with his close followers, among whom was Ōhira Masayoshi, who later became prime minister, he hammered out the new platform: political low posture, separation of politics and economics, and doubling of the national income. This completely emasculated the party program, with its stated goals of constitutional revision and rearmament, and it has seldom been mentioned since. The LDP transformed itself into the likeness of its opposition in one decisive aspect: thenceforward it was the steward of growthmanship. Ali Bhutto of Pakistan was to confer the epithet "economic animal" upon the nation shortly thereafter.

But in the decade of the 1960s, the Japanese were so enamored of the idea of doubling and redoubling their income to "catch up with the West" that it never occurred to them to question this idea. The structure and ideology of the international environment, too, was favorable to growthmanship. A rapid increase in the GNP, "take-off," "modernization," and the like were the goals pursued in earnest by the "capitalist manifesto" and fostered by the United States in the cold war. Herbert Norman's history, which viewed modern Japan as a carry-over of feudalism, was replaced by new scholarship that professed to see in Japanese tradition (for example, in group cohesion) a critical precondition of modernization. At least some part of Japan's modern history would be rejected no more; instead, it had become a model to be emulated by developing countries. On the hundredth anniversary of the

Meiji Restoration in 1968, 23 years after the defeat, there was no objection to celebrating it.

So the decade of the 1960s was the golden age of pacifist commercial democracy. With singleness of purpose and energy seldom paralleled elsewhere in the world, the whole nation pursued the goal of expanding trade and manufacturing. The policy of growthmanship combined with "political low posture" may have been forced on the LDP government at its inception, but it was also a deliberate policy pursued with skill and energy. The architects of Ikeda's policy justified small defense outlays as a booster of economic growth, and the defense budget was allowed to decline from 1.2 percent to 0.8 percent of the GNP during the 1960s. Successive LDP governments, in their dealings with Washington, began to point to the sensitivity of the left on matters of defense in order to stave off U.S. pressures. The United States, for its part, learned not to rock the boat, so as to avert another crisis in 1970, when the Security Treaty was due for an extension. In a way, when the LDP had abandoned its party program in 1960, a period of unconscious collusion between it and the radical-liberal opposition had begun. There would be no more Hatoyamas or Kishis to try to change the course of the country. The initiative would come from outside, in 1971, in the form of the "Nixon shock."

In the meantime, a diffuse sense of nationalistic pride surfaced as the Japanese economy grew by leaps and bounds. Agitation against continued American occupation of Okinawa was one instance, elation over the fastest train in the world was another, and so on. But such pride was channeled by the government into economic activities, to the exclusion of politics. It seemed as a consequence as if the Japanese saw the whole world as a gigantic free market, maintaining its equilibrium of its own accord. They failed to see that the Bretton Woods system was maintained by the deliberate political will of the United States for strategic purposes. For the Japanese, the "invisible hand" was nonexistent because it *was* invisible. Under the formula "separation of politics and economics," Japan sold its products wherever and to whomever it could.[6]

Symbolic of LDP–radical-liberal collaboration in defense of the pacifist commercial regime were the policies of the Three Principles of Nuclear Disarmament and of pegging the defense expenditure at 1 percent of the GNP. These policies were not so much laid down as they were allowed to evolve as extensions of existing public consensus. The three principles, for which Prime Minister Satō Eisaku took credit, state that Japan will not possess, manufacture, or introduce nuclear weapons. Given her history, the first two may be perfectly understandable. But precisely because she does not possess nuclear weapons of her own, Japan is in need of a nuclear umbrella, the presence of which is credible to the Russians to deter them and to the Japanese so they can rest safely. The Satō government, in contrast, made the introduction of nuclear weapons on Japanese soil by the United States a matter of "prior consultation" between the two governments, in accordance with a new provision in the revised Security Treaty of 1960. When Okinawa reverted to Japan in 1972, Satō also succeeded in applying the three principles to the islands.

The U.S. military authority in Japan neither confirms nor denies possession of the weapons; and few people today believe that a submarine or an aircraft carrier removes its nuclear warheads before visiting a Japanese port. The government of Tanaka Kakuei sought to undo the damage done to the credibility of the American nuclear umbrella by the three principles by introducing the so-called 2.5 Principles, leaving the presence of American nuclear weapons on Japanese soil ambiguous; but the attempt was not very successful.

Similar damage to Japan's defense was done when in 1975 Prime Minister Miki Takeo elevated to an express principle what had been merely an existential fact: that Japan's defense expenditure had just happened to hover around 1 percent of her GNP for the previous decade.

Satō Eisaku was later awarded a Nobel Peace Prize for his "initiative" in enunciating the Three Principles of Nuclear Disarmament. Aware that being a brother of Kishi was a liability, Satō, while in office, stressed over and over his support for the Peace Constitution and restrained the revisionist right in the party who derided a Japan awash in the baubles of bourgeois comfort. "The spirit of the new constitution," said Satō, "has become the flesh and blood of the nation."[7] At most, a fine turning, not a revision, was called for—according to Hori Shigeru, one of Satō's close lieutenants—and Hori came up with a justification: Douglas MacArthur himself had realized that there were some excesses in the occupation reforms, for example, in education and domestic security, but he was prevented from readjusting them because of his untimely dismissal.

Hori was a staunch defender of the constitution, and he vowed to eliminate any remnant of "old party influences." But that would have been unnecessary, for prewar party politicians had passed away one after another about the time Satō organized his first cabinet in 1964, and they were no longer a political force in the LDP. The LDP party program of 1955 was dead, and so was the radical-liberals' idea of neutral Japan. No one would dare upset the pacifist commercial democratic regime, dependent upon the United States.

DEFEAT OF THE CONQUEROR

By the close of the 1960s, Japan was the third richest country after the United States and the Soviet Union, and she was well qualified to fulfill the promise made by Yoshida and documented in the Security Treaty of 1951: "Japan will itself increasingly assume responsibility for its own defense against direct and indirect aggression." Many observers had more grandiose expectations. They held out the possibility that a rich Japan would be a powerful Japan. Herman Kahn, author of *The Emerging Japanese Superstate*, and John K. Emmerson, author of *Arms, Yen and Power: The Japanese Dilemma*, may be in this group. Others were vulgar Marxists who assumed that the will to power would come out of economic interest in preserving what Japan had acquired. But they all missed the point. Being able to pay more for defense is quite different from taking the political initiative to do so. That initiative could not have come from within the pacifist regime after Kishi's failure.

The great philosopher Hannah Arendt once stirred up a controversy by accusing the Jewish race of meekly submitting to the Holocaust. A nation may *not* defend itself in the face of an acute threat to its survival. The Jews submitted to the Holocaust, according to her, not because they lacked fear, but because of the absence of political virtue among them. The establishment of the state of Israel, she seemed to suggest, would give Jewry the public arena in which to exercise and nurture political virtue. A key ingredient in that virtue would be a sense of honor and self-respect, a good that only the public can confer. This is a matter of "psychology." The Japanese might have become the Jews of Asia under the Peace Constitution.

Chalmers Johnson, a political scientist at the University of California, Berkeley, has analyzed the same point differently:

> Japan is a "follower nation," economically and politically. This does not mean that Japan is without policies or that it is invariably weak-kneed or unreliable. What it does mean is that Japan's processes of policy formation begin with concrete problems, often created by other actors in the international system, and then go forward to generalized principles and grand strategy, not vice versa. Until quite recently Japanese external policy, both political and economic, has been much more concerned with what we might call operative variables than with parameters and parameter-maintenance. By parameters we mean the structural characteristics of international life, including commercial

life, during a particular period; by operative variables we mean a country's policies for maximizing its own gains within a given parametrical structure.[8]

If the suggestion here is that the Japanese are inherently (for example, culturally) incapable of perceiving parametric questions, however, it would be wrong. Japan *grew* into a follower nation when she decided to leave parameter maintenance entirely to the United States.

Why is it then, we must ask, that Japan should debate about arms today after more than thirty years of inhibition? Why the increase in the nationalistic undercurrent? The problem is acutely political, or politico-psychological. The answer, I suggest, is twofold. First, there was the psychological impact of America's retreat from Vietnam. The Japanese watched in disbelief as the conflict between American doves and hawks got out of hand and created domestic disorder. By the time of the 1970 upheaval in the wake of the Cambodian incursion, Vietnamization of the war seemed irreversible. To see the once mighty conqueror reeling in disarray from a small Asian enemy would certainly have been of some consequence to the Japanese.

Still, it was not their war, and they were undecided as to whether it was a war of communism versus democracy or Asian nationalism versus white men's rule. Then, in one stroke, the Nixon shock of 1971 determined their perception: Vietnam became a war of Asian nationalism even for the conservatives because it was now a war to settle the succession to Japan's former imperial possessions. That Vietnam was a war of Asian nationalism was a foregone conclusion as far as Japan's doves and radical-liberals were concerned, of course. So the transforming impact of the war was greater for the conservatives—even though, torn between two sharply contradictory impulses, they brooded in silence.

The radical-liberals were shrill and articulate in a stereotypical way; they were a carbon copy of the doves, revisionists, and saints of the counterculture in America. But even they could not escape that transforming impact of the war. The pacifist-neutralist sentiment of the Japanese left wing rested on their well-fondled and sickly guilt feeling about Japan's past wars. As the antiwar doves were wont to do everywhere, they jumped at the parallel between Japan's past crime and America's in Vietnam. Since the LDP government stood by America's war effort, they accused the conservatives of committing the same crime a second time in Vietnam—in tandem with the United States. But that, it seems, turned out to be the undoing of their guilt feeling. Previously they had found justification for their neutralism and withdrawal syndrome in their belief that Japan alone in the world was criminal and depraved; hence, to make for a peaceful world, disarmament of Japan would do. Now, on their own admission, there were depravities elsewhere as well. The United States and Japan were equals in sin. He who has not sinned casts the first stone. And yet, in stoning "American imperialism," the Japanese left evidently felt holier.

As the officials of the LDP government parried the abusive invective from the radical-liberals on the war question, they remained strangely taciturn—a sign that they were torn at heart. Dark and powerful emotions seized them as they watched the war. They scoffed at the idea imported from the United States and peddled by Japan's left: that Asian peasant masses armed with bamboo spears have once overcome the imperial Japanese army and will overcome the U.S. army; that Chairman Mao's guerrilla war strategy is invincible; that revolutions in China and Vietnam are internal wars caused by indigenous conditions; and the like. As time went by, they began to see that the motive for erecting the internal war theory was not to account for the objective reality of revolutions in Asia, but to discredit the falling domino theory that sanctioned the cold war. Without discrediting that theory, America could not retreat from Asia. The Japanese conservatives were tempted to tear the internal war theory apart as bunk, but restrained themselves. They could not speak their minds because they knew their thoughts were illegitimate.

Japanese conservatives knew better than to say that "people's wars of liberation" in China and Vietnam were internal wars. They knew better than to say that dominoes do not fall. And indeed, they should have known better: they were on the scene to start these and other nationalist revolutions in Asia. It was they, working under a different constitution, who pushed and toppled the dominoes: the colonial regimes of Britain, France, the Netherlands, and the United States, and such native regimes aligned with them as the Chinese Nationalists. It was Japanese, not Russians or Chinese, who pushed the dominoes over; and it was they who set the torch of nationalism after the collapse of the dominoes. Then neither France nor the United States could restore the status quo ante. It was not until Japan's "Greater East Asian War" had completely undermined the legitimacy of colonial rule that little men dressed in black pajamas could make headway.

But the LDP's senior politicians could not say this with impunity in the pacifist democracy. For was it not the rationale for Japan's war against the United States to say that she had liberated Asia? Yet, did not the legitimacy of the regime they were now defending—with American help—rest on the assumption that Japan's war had been an act of "crime," not "liberation"?

Liberation, said the doves, was what Chairman Mao did; Japan did enslaving.

As time passed and the end appeared near, it became apparent that the United States was moved by a singular desire to liquidate not just the war in Vietnam but everything she had built and done since Pearl Harbor had ended her isolationism. Japan's conservatives understood America's domestic political need for the retreat, of course. Yet they could not but feel that it was utterly reckless and frivolous. The recklessness was not in simply liquidating the defense of Korea, Taiwan, and the alliance with Japan; it was in first imposing American-sponsored regimes in these areas *and* then liquidating them. If the call to "come home, America" was to be taken seriously, however, the whole of America was turning isolationist-revisionist and was questioning by implication the legitimacy of the war in the Pacific! This is what tore the conservative leaders asunder and pulled them in contradictory directions.

Revisionist history written by Japanese writers appeared in flood proportion. America's revisionist history, too, was swiftly translated into Japanese and found an eager audience. Early postwar revisionist imports from America that had been curtly ignored in the past, as if they were misbegotten, were now reread. All of them had a message that George Kennan had captured best:

> It is an ironic fact that today our past objectives in Asia are ostensibly in large measure achieved. The Western powers have lost the last of their special position in China. The Japanese are finally out of China proper and out of Manchuria and Korea as well. The effects of their expulsion from those areas have been precisely what wise and realistic people warned us all along they would be. Today we have fallen heir to the problems and responsibilities the Japanese had faced and borne in the Korean-Manchurian area for nearly half a century, and there is a certain perverse justice in the pain we are suffering from a burden which, when it was borne by others, we held in such low esteem . . .[9]

Kennan was an outstanding example of one school of revisionism that defended geopolitical thinking and criticized the legal-moralistic foundation of American diplomacy.

Then came the ultimate geopolitician of all: President Richard M. Nixon, who had earlier enunciated the doctrine of a pentagonal world of shifting alliances in which an independent Japan would balance herself against the United States, the Soviet Union, China, and Europe. When he delivered the Nixon shock the message was clear, as far as Japan's conservative leaders were concerned. The issue was not Japan's trade surplus, nor was it the wrangle over textiles. The real issue was this: President Nixon was asking Japan to scrap the alliance with the United States and go back to the ways of the 1930s. In a sense, he was vindicating Japan's old continentalism! Coming from the United States, the message seemed utterly absurd; yet she was unmistakably retreating.

There was a sudden surge of pan-Asian sentiment among Japan's conservatives. It had been the monopoly of the pro-Chinese left wing in all those postwar years. Compelled by John Foster Dulles to take Taiwan's side at the San Francisco peace conference, the conservatives had smothered and nearly killed that instinct, for the sake of alliance with the United States. Now it was returning. Hori Shigeru was a mild-mannered man who would countenance constitutional revision only insofar as it was sanctioned by Douglas Mac-Arthur himself. Now the speaker of the lower house, Hori wrote a letter to Premier Chou En-lai. In it he admitted and apologized that his earlier views on China had been mistaken. He went on to say that the history of Asia was the history of domination by white men, and that this domination must be destroyed.[10] The Japanese-U.S. alliance floundered while Japan restored diplomatic relations with China.

What the Nixon shock had left undone, the Arab oil embargo finished off. Japan's ideological environment changed drastically, overnight. Suddenly "take-off," rapid accumulation of GNP points, and the like were so far from being achievements that they had become social crimes. And the Japanese in Southeast Asia were Ugly Japanese for being successful entrepreneurs—even as Chairman Mao posed and was hailed as the "liberator" because he had had the hubris to reject the Western in favor of the "native method." Clearly, it was a time for rethinking basic alternatives. The Nixon shock cast doubt on the wisdom of alliance with the United States, and the oil shock called into question the premise of growthmanship.

There was a sudden doubling in the publications on psycho-cultural analysis of the Japanese, and they replaced revisionist history.[11] It was evident that the Jews of Asia were beginning the search for a new definition of greatness. Japan had graduated from being the Switzerland of Asia, to become an economic power in the 1960s. But there was always a vague dissatisfaction with economism. Fukuda Takeo once derided the period of Prime Minister Satō's incumbency as *Shōwa Genroku*, which translates into something like "baroque in our time." That dissatisfaction pointed to a search for an alternative to the pacifist commercial democratic regime. In 1955 and 1960, Hatoyama and Kishi, respectively, challenged it with their ill-defined and abortive scheme. Japan's search for a new role will recur to their basic motive: to restore the primacy of politics over economics.

The search should have begun in 1975, when Saigon fell. But the only men who could sponsor such a movement, the leaders of the LDP, were in the heat of the Lockheed scandal, the biggest crisis since the founding of their party in 1955. A former prime minister was in jail, and a weak caretaker government was drifting. It was not until the LDP had retrenched, regrouped, and gone into a new surge that Fukuda took the initiative to raise the issue of defense. He is a close follower of Kishi.

FRIEND OR REVANCHIST?

A question may naturally arise: will the search for a new role take Japan on the path to revanchism? Will not Japan, no longer believing in the verdict of the Tokyo Trial in toto, be bent on revenge against the United States? There is, to be sure, a specific circumstance—adumbrated above—under which the Japanese people would have come to resent the United States. Suppose the United States had abandoned herself to the impulse to retreat all the way to Hawaii, justifying that retreat with the Nixon Doctrine. Suppose also that the United States had simply scuttled the defense of Korea, and that a war had broken out. The United States might have persuaded herself that the retreat was necessary. But the Japanese would have seen it as the frivolous act of an irresponsible power. Forced either to fight to retake Korea or to join China for protection, they might have felt vindicated in their old continentalism. Fortunately, none of this happened, because America's recovery from defeat was much swifter than Japan's.

Will Japan be revanchist nevertheless? This question will be touched on as a part of some larger issues in the concluding chapter. But since I have dealt so much here with questions of war guilt, that issue must be concluded. The Pacific War will always be a sensitive matter between the United States and Japan; but it cannot be glossed over, because how we view the war will affect our bearings in the future. This is not an academic question. For instance, Japan's SDFs are still using a troop indoctrination manual that stresses the United Nations but avoids any reference to past wars. This will have to change. As Samuel Huntington has pointed out, an army without tradition will not be reliable in battle.

For the sake of continued friendship, the two countries would be well advised to work out a mutually acceptable view of World War II. Such an effort, a revision of revision, is already under way among academics of both nationalities, and it should be encouraged.[12] In the meantime, what is the true feeling today of a middle-of-the-road Japanese about the war? In 1969, a leading newspaper held a symposium of leaders of all the political parties on the subject of Japan's security. The following exchange took place between Miyamoto Kenji, chairman of the Japan Communist party, and Tanaka Kakuei, who shortly thereafter became prime minister.

> MIYAMOTO: The Security Treaty, the Okinawa question, and the like, to which you have just referred, have all come about as the result of World War II . . . I should like to ask how you would characterize the world war and the war in China. According to your campaign manual, we went to war because the nation became overconfident. But then, on the other hand . . . you say that the mistake was in losing . . .
>
> TANAKA: . . . I do not want to dig up things that have gone down in history. Moreover . . . this is not a question for partisan debate. I don't think World War II was such a simple war in the history of the Japanese nation. During the occupation it was simply regarded as a war of aggression by Japan, and that was that. But it was not that simple . . . At that time, we Japanese had virtually no natural resources. There were some hundred million of us then, and when we tried to obtain cheap imports we were kicked around by the high tariffs. We tried to immigrate elsewhere, and we were slapped with exclusion. Our export goods were discriminated against. Didn't we hit the very bottom in the Depression? Still, we went on to assault Imphal, Guadalcanal, and Sydney, and tried to take one-third of the earth. That was aggression. That was going too far. But after the Sino-Japanese War, everything that came thereafter including the days when the Japanese nation was spitting blood—"Was that not a war of aggression?" you say in one sentence, and demand my answer. That's very difficult.[13]

An intelligent American—not a wide-eyed revisionist—in the post-Vietnam era may realize that the verdict of the Far Eastern Military Tribunal had all the one-sidedness of victor's justice. It was to Japan what the verdict of the counterculture has been to America and her history. To say, therefore, that a majority of the Japanese today do not believe in that verdict is far from saying that they feel they were simply right, or that they seek revenge. What they feel about the origin of the war is probably very close to what Tanaka Kakuei has expressed above.

Moreover, the most salient development in Japanese public opinion since the fall of Saigon in 1975 has been an *increase* rather than a decrease in friendly feeling and even sympathy for America. Many factors can be adduced to account for this. For instance, the left could heretofore "kick the United

States around," so to speak, without fear of losing her protection. This is no longer the case. The Japanese people are also aware of the important place accorded them by the successors of President Nixon in American strategic thought about East Asia; and they may feel uplifted by it.

But the most important factor may be one that the Japanese are not clearly aware of. In all the postwar years, the Japanese have harbored hidden resentment toward their former conqueror, who has been ahead of them in almost anything they have done, be it in entrepreneurship, inventiveness, or, not the least, warmaking. In this view, America's bungling and subsequent humiliation in a war of succession to Japan's former possession might have constituted a comeuppance. The way some conservative Japanese cheered on the Vietcong after the Nixon shock suggests that the Vietcong had become their proxy against white men—even though they knew full well that that was an illusion. In a way, Hanoi's victory constituted that perverse justice that George Kennan spoke of, and it wiped the slate clean of war-related emotion. Today the Japanese people are seeing America for exactly what she is: a true friend and ally in the turbulent and treacherous world.

LIMITS OF PACIFISM

What can be concluded from the foregoing? First, Japan is still a pacifist country. Three attempts to change that, two from within and one from without, have not altered that fact. But the third one may have started an internal response that could grow into a secular trend away from the pacifist character. In the meantime, Japan is in a state of tension. To return to the tripartite division of the Japanese body-politic—the supporters of neutrality, of minimum self-defense resting on an unequal alliance with the United States, and the advocates of security plus honor—the first group may dwindle further and the third may grow. But it is my belief that the present regime will persist until Japan is threatened from without.

In the meantime, below are the limits beyond which Japan will not go in matters of national defense.

—Defensive defense. Japan will not send her troops abroad for forward deployment. Public opinion in a democracy at war cannot be gauged by what it is in peacetime; once "Pearl Harbor" is struck, anything is possible. But until then Japan will not commit her troops to Korea or dispatch destroyers to escort her own merchant marine abroad. This means that Japan cannot take part in a regional or collective security arrangement.

—The Three Principles of Nuclear Disarmament. In spite of invidious speculations, Japan has ratified the Nuclear Nonproliferation Treaty, thus reaffirming the Three Principles. What is probably in effect today is 2.5 principles whereby the Japanese government raises no objection to covert introduction of nuclear weapons onto Japanese territory. This is as it should be.

—Some upper ceiling in the total defense budget. The current limit of 1 percent of the GNP obviously has no rationale, and when the LDP increases its parliamentary strength it can raise the ceiling. On the other hand, Japan will not increase her current annual defense budget of $10 billion to $50 or $60 billion (5 and 6 percent of the GNP, respectively) without fundamentally altering her character.

—A ban on the sale of weapons abroad. Producing weapons only for national use, Japan cannot enjoy economies of scale, and her weapons are expensive; hence the government is constrained to buy from abroad, which retards the nation's research and development. This ban is under attack from the business community.

Finally, there is the issue of a free ride. Japan is not "free riding" on American defense. If she were literally free riding, that is, if she were in a state of unarmed neutrality, the United States would nonetheless be making a considerable effort to keep her from falling under Soviet influence. Japan is valuable to the United States with or without her contribution to defense. But it so happens that Japan's defense budget ranks seventh in the world: this is not a free ride. On the other hand, it is clearly a cheap ride, and it has been so since about 1960.

But cheap or free, Japan has not contrived to take this posture out of rational calculation or with a view to taking unfair advantage of the United States, as many slanderous, malign critics imply. For the most part, Japan has not been able to help being what she is or taking the policy that she has taken. But of all the limits of pacifism, the fiscal one is the most susceptible to change. Japan could pay 2 percent of her GNP for defense, for instance, without changing her pacifist character. But the only way to eliminate the cheap ride altogether is to create a Gaullist Japan, complete with *force de frappe*.

CHAPTER THREE

Politics of the Defense Controversy

Phase one of the defense controversy that is the subject of this study was initiated by Prime Minister Fukuda Takeo in early 1978, when he seized on the question of the SDFs as an issue in his bid for the LDP presidency in a party primary. The controversy seemed to subside toward the end of the year when the primary ended in an upset victory for Ōhira Masayoshi. But that was not to be. Public debate flared up with renewed vigor in 1979; it now seems likely to continue as long as the state of Japan's defense remains archaic and threadbare. In posing defense questions, Fukuda's immediate aim was to secure public acceptance of the SDFs as they now exist, that is, with all the constitutional and political restrictions. By design and in its effect, the debate at this stage amounted to a public hearing and acclamation of the government's new defense policy, which had been laid down in October 1976 but which did not register on public consciousness because the country was in the grip of the Lockheed scandal.

Fukuda succeeded in his aim, and thereby demonstrated that talking about the state of national defense was no longer dangerous politically. At this point the floodgate sprang open: all the discontent and doubt about the government's defense posture surfaced. What had just won acclamation is now being subjected to deepening criticism in phase two. In tracing the almost inevitable progression of the controversy from phase one to phase two, I hope to direct attention to an agonizing dilemma: efforts to improve national defense necessarily run into constitutional barriers.

Defense is an acutely political, though no longer a moral-legal issue in Japan, and the timing and manner in which it was debated underscored this point. LDP leaders and the defense bureaucracy are keeping a close ear to the ground in a time of far-reaching political change. On the basis of close collaboration with their counterparts in Washington—a veritable "transnational bureaucratic alliance"—they are keeping pace with the emerging consensus, with mixed results. Accordingly, the defense controversy will be related here to the context of recent political developments.

The highlight of those developments is the decline of the "1955 system," so-called, and the "rightward shift" of public sentiment from the postwar pacifist left to the center-right. The 1955 system was that rigid and semi-ideological division between the ruling LDP and the radical-liberals led by the strong Socialist party. The cornerstone of that division was the question of the Japan-U.S. Security Treaty and the SDFs, and the anti–Security Treaty struggle of 1960 was the culmination of this division. Both the LDP and the Socialists have been in slow decline at the polls since their founding in 1955, but the irrelevance of the issue that divided them did not become apparent until America's decline was driven home to the Japanese mind by the Nixon shock and the fall of Saigon.

Fukuda's tactic of a limited offensive to win public acceptance of the SDFs was in fact an idea hatched by his predecessors as early as 1968. In October 1976 a new defense policy embodying that idea—entitled the "National Defense Program Outline" (hereafter referred to as Outline)—was adopted by cabinet decision. The defense controversy could have started then but for the diversion created by two events: first, Japan had not yet recovered economically or psychologically from the disarray caused by the oil embargo and the recession; second, the LDP was just then fighting for its life in the biggest crisis in its history and was in no shape to take on another controversy.

THE LOCKHEED FIASCO

The 1976 revelation that President Nixon had leaned on Prime Minister Tanaka Kakuei (Satō's successor) to sell aircraft manufactured by a multi-national located in Nixon's home state of California, and that Tanaka was taking bribes for doing Nixon's bidding, struck Japan like a thunderbolt. Perhaps it was an isolated incident. But to many Japanese it seemed a necessary culmination of the series of jolting shocks to the pacifist-commercial order and the American connection that the LDP represented. The fact that the latest jolt had once again originated in Washington suggested a parallel between it and the Nixon shock. Although some admired America's ability to rectify political corruption, others inferred that there was a price to be paid for too close a collaboration with the United States. Certainly the ability of the American body politic to shift gear in mid-course and turn on itself, was a reminder to her allies to maintain a degree of reserve and autonomy. For having failed to do so, the LDP was so compromised that it seemed unable to survive.

Our interest here is not with the Lockheed incident itself but with its impact on the already fluid political alignment in Japan. For the first time since its founding, the LDP was in serious danger of disintegration. This had the obvious tonic effect on the opposition. The man entrusted with the task of saving the day for the conservative party, Miki Takeo, moreover, did not command the allegiance of the more important factions of the LDP and he was forced to drift until he was retired in the wake of a defeat in the lower house election of 1976. Just prior to the election, a small group of young LDP members bolted the party to form the New Liberal Club (NLC), dedicated to the goal of reconstructing the conservative party. The NLC did surprisingly well among young urban voters, whereas the LDP lost its majority by a slim margin.

It seems in retrospect, however, that, having chastised the ruling party, the voters withheld themselves from the prospect of living under a radical-liberal or coalition government. There was another critical election, for the upper house in 1977, that showed a surprising result. The LDP, now led by Fukuda Takeo, barely managed to hold its own; the NLC did rather poorly, and the Socialists suffered a disaster. The upshot was that in both houses of parliament the LDP was on uncertain footing, but the opposition seemed to have lost the momentum they appeared to be enjoying at the height of the Lockheed upheaval.

The behavior of Japanese voters in the past several years does not lend itself to any theoretically satisfying analysis. The much-celebrated 1976 election cannot justly be termed a "Lockheed election." The LDP's loss was small and within the range predictable from its long-term decline. If there had been an alternative center party, the electorate might have "thrown the rascals out." But 1976–77 saw Japan still recovering from inflation, recession, and a trade deficit caused by the oil price hike. The voters might have felt that they had no choice but to stay with the experienced party. It is also possible that the structure of Japanese voters of rural and/or conservative background is such that they are to some degree immune to changing issues. For instance: Tanaka was returned with an unprecedented majority.

The LDP, resting on the cooperation of the Fukuda-Ōhira factions, was intent on revitalizing itself. Some measures, long sought but never realized, were agreed upon, among them the system of electing the party president and hence the prime minister by vote of party members both in and out of parliament. Between the two main contenders for the post, Fukuda and

Ōhira, two different readings of the LDP's future became discernible. Fukuda professed to see in the result of the 1977 election a turning point for the party's fortunes; hence he was less willing to solicit the cooperation of minor parties in legislative programs. Ōhira, on the other hand, felt that the smallness of the government majority dictated a more conciliatory posture and the need for greater compromises. The two began to shop around for issues on which to conduct the campaign. As a mechanism for the presidential election, the LDP set the goal of recruiting 1.5 million party members.

The JSP's recent setback, combined with the rather solicitous government resting on a slim majority, has had an impact on the opposition that has been at once sobering and tantalizing. The radical-liberal parties have shed their doctrinaire stances and begun to look more seriously at the give-and-take of the parliamentary process. That includes even the JSP, whose chairman resigned in the wake of the unsuccessful election and was replaced by new leaders, trying—though rather halfheartedly—to build a party of one million members, a number too large to be recruited solely on ideological grounds. If all the parties out of power can agree on a common program, they will be in a position to frustrate the government, especially since they hold the majority in many critical parliamentary committees. That is what the JSP and the JCP are trying to achieve, in vain. But the issue that once united the opposition, that is, the Security Treaty and the SDFs, has ceased to be an issue since 1975.

The government has an incentive to adopt a divide and rule tactic by cultivating temporary allies among the more agreeable opposition parties through offers of concessions. Thus, a split appeared in the opposition, with the JSP and the JCP on one side and the NLC, the Democratic Socialist party (a counterpart of the social democratic parties in Western Europe, which broke away from the JSP in 1960), the Clean Government party, and the Social Democratic League (another, tiny splinter from the JSP in 1977) on the government's side. The NLC is a conservative party, but the remaining three would rather call themselves center than simply radical-liberal parties.

The situation is clearly transitional; it portends further changes in the future, including a possible decline of the JSP into a minor party. But the change in the domestic power relationship reflects as well as reinforces the shift in public opinion. In the past only the DSP and the NLC supported the Security Treaty and the SDFs. Then, in early 1978, the Clean Government party announced that in order to pave the way for a "center-conservative coalition," it was prepared to endorse the alliance and the SDFs. In the decision, this pro-Chinese party was clearly influenced by China's unsolicited advice on stronger defense for Japan. Later in the year, internal opposition developed against the collusion with the LDP, and the party has retracted the change. But it is my judgment that the Clean Government party will come around soon.

The Social Democratic League split from the Marxist-dominated JSP in 1977. It is now formally committed to gradual "decomposition" of the military alliance with the United States and its eventual replacement by a new treaty emphasizing cultural and economic ties; and slow reduction by stages of the SDF's to a constabulary force. But the point here seems to be that the final state is put off so far into the future that the League is prepared to live with the status quo in the meantime.

The Communists are less doctrinaire than the Socialists in Japan; and during the 1976 election campaign, Chairman Miyamoto of the JCP created a stir by not attacking the Security Treaty and the SDFs. It is possible for the JCP to advance in the future to the same point at which Eurocommunism now stands with respect to the North Atlantic Treaty Organization.

The JSP has been the laughing stock of the country lately because of its utter incompetence and confusion in the foreign policy area. Ever since its founding, the JSP has agitated for friendly relations with China and against the Security Treaty. But once China had established a government-to-government relationship with Japan, she began to neglect the JSP. As if that were not enough, Teng Hsiao-p'ing began in his usual style to criticize the JSP's opposition to the Security Treaty. The Chinese and Vietnamese invasion of their neighbors in 1979 left the Socialists speechless, for they obviously could not resolve the differences between the pro-Chinese wing and the pro-Soviet (hence pro-Vietnamese) wing.

In late 1978 the JSP laid down this formal position: because the Security Treaty had been directed at the Chinese threat, but because a friendly Japan-China relationship had been established, the Security Treaty must be scrapped in two stages; the SDFs, too, must be reduced (in three stages) and eventually liquidated, after a "relatively protracted period." But the party is now in favor of establishing and sitting on a parliamentary committee on defense. (The Japanese parliament has not had one until now!)

But the forces pushing the Socialists to the right would not relent, and a little over a year later they were forced not only to acknowledge the permanence of the Security Treaty, but also bolt the united front with the Communists. I shall return to this matter in a summary of the latest political developments below.

FUKUDA AND BILLY MITCHELL

It was in the context of the thaw on military taboos that the first race to determine who would be the LDP's president got under way in early 1978. There were three early contenders: Fukuda, Ōhira, and Nakasone. Fukuda was in an expansive mood about the prospects for the party's resurgence; Ōhira chose a cautious posture. Fukuda's faction contains the largest number of MPs belonging to the Blue Storm Society, a group of hard-liners on domestic and foreign issues. Nakasone, to the right of the other two, has a populist inclination. Both he and Fukuda saw the turning to the right (*migi-senkai*) in public sentiment and decided to make an issue out of defense problems.

The election was an intraparty affair for card-carrying members, who are more conservative than the general public. Among the party's rank and file there was a surge of self-confidence, as the value of the yen climbed and the government's "headache" of reducing the trade surplus continued. "Economically we are unbeatable," said one LDP politician. But as in the case of the presidential primary in the United States—after which the Japanese election was modeled—this election was to be a forum for educating the public, and all three contenders (later joined by a fourth) addressed themselves to the country at large.

One report tells of the origin of Fukuda's campaign strategy as follows. Early in January he was visited by an influential leader of the party and a confidant, and the two talked roughly thus:

> VISITOR: There is something I've been thinking seriously about these days, as parties multiply and the opposition draws near the ruling party in parliamentary strength. It is good that differences between the two sides have diminished. But in the absence of tension, the government loses the will to see its policies through, and political responsibilities are blurred.
>
> FUKUDA: What do you propose?
>
> VISITOR: Economic problems are of course important. But at the same time, the government and the LDP must face the problems of the future. They must vigorously hammer out an autonomous line, and in doing so try to restructure conservative politics.[14]

Shortly thereafter Fukuda delivered his "State of the Union," in which he expressed his hope that defense questions would be put to wide-ranging and constructive debate. That Fukuda, a seasoned politician, apparently felt that he stood to gain politically by raising the defense issue amounted to a stunning upset of a postwar taboo.

Then the fireworks began, in parliamentary interpellations. Government officials of the defense and other agencies, and later the prime minister himself, stated one after the other that Japan is not constitutionally barred from possessing thermonuclear weapons, neutron bombs, cruise missiles, bacteriological weapons, aircraft carriers for anti-submarine warfare, and so on. They averred that a constitutionally legitimate means of self-defense is relative to the development of science and technology. An intercontinental ballistic missile, according to them, falls into the category of war capability and is still unconstitutional; but some types of nuclear weapons are not. Nevertheless, they said, Japan shall continue to refrain from possessing nuclear weapons because of the *government's policy* of the Three Principles of Nuclear Disarmament—not because of the constitution.

What was surprising in all this was not only that the government had made the statements, but also that nothing of political consequence happened: no head rolled, as surely it would have rolled ten years before. As late as 1968, fear of opposition had forced the government to remove the bombsight and air-refueling equipment from the new F-4 Phantoms it had purchased from the United States. Then Fukuda and the LDP decided to have the government sponsor a National Founders Day holiday, and Fukuda himself visited Yasukuni Shrine (Japan's Arlington Cemetery and Tomb of the Unknown Soldier combined)in his official capacity as prime minister. As Japan's prime ministers would not pay homage to war dead in the recent past, Fukuda had to defend himself in parliament against left-wing protests.

Nakasone took to the campus of Tokyo University, the citadel of student radicalism and violence in the 1960s, and delivered a speech demanding the repeal of Article IX of the constitution, expressly to legitimize the status of the SDFs. To the chagrin of the "doves," the students roared their applause. A pacifist press laconically reported that Tokyo University's students are indeed "elite" and vote like their wealthy parents.

National debate on defense was on; and it reached a new high in July, when Japan produced her own Billy Mitchell. Kurisu Hiro'omi, a four-star general and chairman of the Joint Staff Council (the counterpart of the U.S. Joint Chiefs of Staff), had been distraught over the dismal state of Japan's defense readiness for some years. Apparently he had been waiting for a good opportunity to take the issue to the public. He saw that opportunity come his way in January. It took courage to go public, for, as he admitted later, to do so was wholly alien to Japan's bureaucratic tradition. In a magazine article in

January, Kurisu pointed out the bankruptcy of the concept of defensive defense.[15] But the article escaped public notice.

He tried again in July and was duly noticed. This time he called attention to the fact that, as things stand today, SDF personnel cannot take defensive action against hostile intruders unless the prime minister first orders the SDFs mobilized. For twenty years, Kurisu said, uniformed officers had been asking for a government ruling or for legislation to clarify the limits of permissible action in an emergency, and for twenty years they had been ignored. In a future emergency, therefore, SDF local commanders might have to shoot first and ask for permission later, in what he termed a translegal act.

Pacifist media were delighted to trounce the bogey of the Kwantung Army. The Fukuda cabinet and the LDP showed great sympathy for Kurisu but felt bound to dismiss him. But he had accomplished his purpose.

In November 1978 Fukuda lost his presidential bid in a surprise upset. Political analysts agree that his defeat should be ascribed to the factional balance of power and not to the defense issue. Primarily for the purpose of the campaign, Ōhira soft-pedaled that issue. Although it is true that Ōhira is less inclined to be combative, there is no basic difference of philosophy or policy preference between him and Fukuda. Besides, Fukuda's achievement in the defense area had so far been incremental; he was content to let Nakasone agitate for constitutional revision without committing himself to it. Even if he had stayed on, Japan's course would have been more or less the same.

But the impact of the presidential campaign on politics itself is worth noting because it will affect future defense policy. Forced by the Lockheed fiasco to accept it, old-fashioned senior politicians—including the octogenarian Fukuda—nevertheless did not take kindly to what they regarded as the legacy of Miki's reformist zeal: a presidential primary, American style! But to their surprise, the election turned out to be a booster for conservative causes; and these politicians are now firmly committed to keeping the institution. The moral of its success seems to be that a bit of populism is what Japanese voters were looking for. The idea of participating in the election of the prime minister, in exchange for the payment of small party dues, energized the rank and file of the LDP—which swelled to 1.5 million, as targeted. This promises to relieve the party from its heavy reliance on business contributions. The spectacle of Fukuda bowing before the popular mandate and stepping down added to the party members' sense of self-importance, and they are not likely to relinquish their newly acquired power. There are drawbacks to the presidential elections, such as the nationalization of party factions. But the system is, on balance, clearly desirable, and Ōhira has vowed to use it to build a party of three million.

Prime minister Ōhira had assumed his office at a time when major changes were taking place in Japan's local politics as well. In a series of mayoral and gubernatorial elections in 1978 and early 1979, well-entrenched Socialist incumbents in Kyoto, Yokohama, Okinawa, Tokyo, and Osaka—to name only the most critical areas—were dislodged by LDP challengers. To the elated LDP leadership, this was the final confirmation of its hope that the party had put the Lockheed crisis behind. Ōhira decided that the time was ripe for an attempt to regain the parliamentary supremacy in a new context. The bumptious mood of the otherwise circumspect prime minister was indicated by the fact that in calling the lower house election for October 1979, he predicted (as did most leading newspapers, by the way) that the LDP would win as many as 271 seats, which would give him an absolute mastery over the 511-seat house. As he was to regret later, he stood on a platform of tax increase to reduce government debts.

The election results (see Table 1), in the order of significance, are 1) another clear-cut defeat for the Socialists (who lost 16 seats out of 123 won in the last election); 2) gains by two center parties presumably at the expense of the Socialists; 3) an ambiguous outcome for the LDP (which lost one seat while gaining by 2.8 percent in party vote over the last election); and 4) a gain by the Communists that is more apparent than real because it comes from skillful apportioning of stable party vote.

For some forty days following Ōhira's nonvictory at the polls, Japan saw a tempest in a teapot: he was blamed for not producing the landslide victory he had promised. The anti-Ōhira factions led by Fukuda demanded that the prime minister assume responsibility for the "defeat" and stand down. The opposing sides could not settle their differences within the party, and they took the fight to the parliament—where Ōhira was endorsed.

This episode is of interest to us only because it is indicative of the further decline of the 1955 system. When Fukuda had failed to win majority support for himself in the LDP, he asked the Democratic Socialists if they would vote for him in the parliament, thereby forming a coalition government.[16] Fukuda was rebuffed and returned to the LDP's fold. But it is apparent that on key issues such as Japan's international orientation, the differences that used to separate the LDP from the bulk of the opposition have disappeared, and that preconditions necessary for political realignment now exist. Surprisingly, however, the LDP has recovered a semblance of unity. So, the two most likely

TABLE 1
The Lower House Election of 1979

		seats won in 1979	seats won in 1976
right[a]	Liberal Democratic party	248	249
↑	New Liberal Club	4	17
	Democratic Socialist party	35	29
	Clean Government party	57	55
	Social Democratic League	2	—[b]
↓	Japan Socialist party	107	123
left	Japan Communist party	39	17
	Independent	19[c]	21
	total	511	511

[a]Placement of a party on the right-left spectrum is highly impressionistic and tentative.
[b]The Social Democratic League split off from the JSP in 1977.
[c]Of the 19 independents, 14 are conservative, including Tanaka Kakuei, who left the LDP because of the involvement in the Lockheed affair.

forms of realignment at the moment are 1) the LDP's coalition with a minor center party and 2) the coming together of all center parties in an attempt to displace the LDP government.

The second form began to materialize in late 1979, when the Socialists were pressured into parting company with the JCP as a precondition for negotiating a coalition agreement with the Clean Government party and the DSP, previously a right-wing of the JSP. The pressure came from Sōhyō (General Council of Trade Unions), on which the JSP has depended almost entirely for funds as well as for votes, in the form of a threat to disown the JSP unless it saved itself from further decline. The more radical of the two union councils, Sōhyō itself has recently been fighting an uphill battle against the conservative competitor.

No doubt the JSP's break with the past will not be a clean one because of the presence of die-hard Marxist-Leninists on the left, but the direction in which it has began to move is quite apparent. On the domestic front, it will have to abandon the posture of being a class party and become instead a national party much like the social democratic parties of Western Europe. The united front with the Communists, which was the backbone of the radical-liberal coalition, is now dead. On the SDF question, the Socialists are still clinging to the time-honored goal of their eventual reduction and reorganization. But the party has made an important concession on the Security Treaty: whereas it used to insist on unilateral termination of the treaty once it formed a government, it now agrees to make the termination conditional on unanimous consent of both Japan and the United States—thus conceding a veto power to the latter.

Because the LDP's alleged "defeat"—rather than the JSP's real defeat—has made so much news, an impression has been created that the "rightward shift" initiated by Fukuda has given way to "centrist politics" of the Socialists. This is a superficial view in my judgment. Japan is still moving to the right. It is doing so by zigzag or dialectically: Fukuda initiated the move but was pushed aside; then the initiative passed to the opposition, which is moving one step closer to the LDP. Next time the LDP tries to go further than asking for public acceptance of the SDFs, for instance, it may very well succeed. Since the anti–Security Treaty upheaval of 1960, when Japan had fully articulated herself as a pacifist commercial democracy, the LDP has been secretly colluding with the radical-liberal opposition. The time has come for the LDP to end that collusion because the opposition itself is casting away the Marxist-dominated past.

With a bit of luck and proper leadership, the LDP can still grow because it is full of life and vitality. Its factionalism does present a problem. But, as James Madison observed (*Federalist Papers*, no. 10): "Liberty is to faction what air is to fire, an aliment without which it instantly expires. But it could not be less folly to abolish liberty, which is essential to political life, because it nourishes faction, than it would be to wish the annihilation of air, which is essential to animal life, because it imparts to fire its destructive agency."

There is an additional perspective on factionalism. LDP factionalism is the only instance in which Japanese politicians exhibit audacity, willfulness, and daring. Having abstained from pursuit of power or prestige abroad, they have nevertheless preserved their political quality in a small domestic niche. The contrary is true of the pacifist opposition. Its past impotence stemmed from its unwillingness to sacrifice ideological purity in the interest of acquiring power, as witness the Democratic Socialists' refusal to accept Fukuda's bid for a coalition government. With the emergence of an effective opposition, however, factionalism may serve as a foundation for healthy partisanship between two parties that alternate in power. This augurs well for republican freedom in Japan.

As an index of the current state of Japanese public opinion on matters of national security, here is the result of a poll taken in November 1978—when phase one of the defense controversy was about to subside.[17]

QUESTION: Do you agree or disagree with the proposal for a constitutional amendment that would formally enable Japan to possess armed forces?

> Agree: 15%
> Disagree: 71%

Other: 5%
No answer: 9%

QUESTION: Do you think the Security Treaty concluded by Japan and the United States serves our interest?

Yes: 49%
No: 13%
Neither: 22%
Other: 2%
No answer: 14%

QUESTION: When worse comes to worst, do you think the United States will seriously defend Japan?

Yes: 20%
No: 56%
Other: 8%
No answer: 16%

QUESTION: What do you think is the most important factor that safeguards Japan?—choose among the following:

Economic power: 20%
Peace Constitution: 15%
Patriotism: 13%
SDFs   2%
U.S. support   2%
Peace diplomacy: 42%
Other: 2%
No answer: 4%

QUESTION: With which country do you think Japan should maintain the most friendly relations in the future?

The United States: 29%
China: 23%
The Soviet Union: 3%
Other: 27%
No answer: 18%

The answers are full of contradictions. The Japanese do not have much confidence in American protection, yet they are overwhelmingly against constitutional revision. The notion that peace diplomacy rather than U.S. support safeguards Japan is so transparently false as to be disturbing. The main conclusion to be drawn from this poll is that the Japanese public at large—in contradistinction to the "elite"—is simply interested in the status quo, including the SDFs and alliance with the United States.

What distinguishes today's Japan from what she was prior to 1971, however, is not that the common man is still caught up in the inertia of the pacifist past, but that a small minority of the elite feel free at last to raise systemic or parametric questions. The ferment among opinion leaders is not confined to the military dimension, but is part of a much broader current. It is a quiet ferment because no acute crisis is in sight that would expose any glaring defect in the status quo. For a country that is doing so competently economically, however, the pervasive sense of discomfort and unease is striking.

But that seems to be precisely the point: Japan's race to catch up with the West in material well-being has been won, and the nation is poised in search of a new goal. The Japanese are aware that the view of *Japan as Number One* (to borrow the title of Ezra Vogel's book, which became an instant best-seller in Japan) may be true in some respects; but it is only number two or three in others.

Indeed, the ferment arises from the tension between Japan as number one and Japan as a military dependency of another power. As yet, the Japanese are not clearly aware that the tension may develop into a search for a new regime. Already, however, a far-reaching consensus on domestic order has emerged that is embraced by the left no less than by the conservatives. First, Japan no longer needs to pile creature comfort upon creature comfort. This leaves her with symbolic, as opposed to material, values as a goal. It has become common to hear people speak of Japan's "international responsibility"—though few seem to realize that this is a synonym for national prestige.

Second, it is realized by left and right that democracy has been distorted under the aegis of economism into a system in which the interests of the part overwhelm that of the whole. The public is beginning to find it intolerable, for instance, that the government cannot even build a decent international airport for the capital and that it succumbs meekly to hijackers. To restore the public realm to its rightful place, Japan will necessarily move in the direction of a stronger government—one that will cast aside the LDP's time-honored formula of political low posture.

THE STANDARD DEFENSE FORCE CONCEPT

As noted above, the defense controversy falls into two phases. Phase one ran the whole length of 1978, and Fukuda and LDP politicians monopolized the stage. Aside from staking his political fortunes in the presidential primary on the rightward shift of public sentiment, Fukuda sought public acceptance of the SDFs. In fact, however, this goal had been on the LDP's drawing board since the last days of the Satō government in 1972. In order to compel the radical-liberal opposition to acquiesce in the existence of the SDFs, the LDP, assisted by the Defense bureaucracy, had put together a sugarcoated pill—a political halfway measure—on defense that the opposition found difficult to reject: namely, Japan's new defense posture embodied in Outline, a cabinet decision of October 1976 (by Miki). Fukuda delayed his effort to win public approval of Outline until 1978. When he found the public receptive, he introduced its counterpart in late November: the Draft Guideline for Japan-U.S. Defense Cooperation (hereafter referred to as Guideline). Guideline had its inception in Miki's visit to Washington in August 1975, three months after the fall of Saigon. But as far as Outline was concerned, Fukuda put before the public a policy conceived at the height of the LDP's collusion with pacifism and in the early phase of détente. When the uniformed officers of the Defense bureaucracy saw that neither Outline nor Guideline provoked the opposition, their discontent with the former suddenly surfaced and ushered in phase two of the controversy. A look at the official defense posture will show why.

Pursuant to Basic Policies for National Defense, adopted in May 1957, Japan carried out three defense buildup plans between 1958 and 1971 (see Table 2). Although the share of the defense budgets in total GNP was rather small and constant during those years, the budgets kept increasing nevertheless because the GNP was growing fast. Too, those were the years of unquestioned LDP parliamentary supremacy, and the government enjoyed relative freedom in enacting the minuscule defense programs.

But in 1971–72, troubles began to mount for the conservatives. The Nixon shock compromised the Satō government, and the People's Republic of China let it be known that it would deal only with a successor government in Tokyo. Intra-LDP maneuvers for succession were under way, and the opposition, too, was fishing for an issue on which to challenge the government. Then a series of events prompted the opposition to seize on the defense issue: the midair collision of an Air SDF jet-trainer with a passenger plane; the joint Satō-Nixon communiqué of January 1972 committing Japan to the regional security of Taiwan and South Korea; and not the least, the budget request for the fourth defense buildup plan submitted by the ambitious and hawkish Defense Minister Nakasone.

Even before Satō was replaced by Tanaka in July 1972, a deliberation had started among LDP leaders that addressed the questions raised by the opposition: How many more defense buildup plans were in the works? How far did the government intend to expand the SDFs? Did not the Peace Constitution imply a limit to the permissible size of the army? The government saw a glimmer of hope in that the opposition was raising questions about the extent

TABLE 2
Defense Capability Development

			1st Buildup Plan (1958–1960) — 170,000 men	2nd Buildup Plan (1962–1966) — 171,500 men	3rd Buildup Plan (1967–1971) — 179,000 men	4th Buildup Plan — 180,000 men
GSDF		Self-Defense official quota / Units deployed regionally in peacetime	6 Divisions; 3 Composite Brigades	12 Divisions	12 Divisions	12 Divisions; 1 Composite Brigade
	Basic Units	Mobile Operation Units	1 Mechanized Combined Brigade; 1 Tank Regiment; 1 Artillery Brigade; 1 Airborne Brigade; 1 Training Brigade	1 Mechanized Division; 1 Tank Regiment; 1 Artillery Brigade; 1 Airborne Brigade; 1 Training Brigade	1 Mechanized Division; 1 Tank Regiment; 1 Artillery Brigade; 1 Airborne Brigade; 1 Training Brigade; 1 Helicopter Brigade	1 Mechanized Division; 1 Tank Brigade; 1 Artillery Brigade; 1 Airborne Brigade; 1 Training Brigade; 1 Helicopter Brigade
		Low-Altitude Ground-to-Air Missile Units	—	2 Anti-Aircraft Artillery Battalions	4 Anti-Aircraft Artillery Groups (another group being prepared)	8 Anti-Aircraft Artillery Groups
MSDF	**Basic Units**	Anti-Submarine Surface-Ship Units (for mobile operation)	3 Escort Flotillas	3 Escort Flotillas	4 Escort Flotillas	4 Escort Flotillas
		Anti-Submarine Surface-Ship Units (Regional District Units)	5 Divisions	5 Divisions	10 Divisions	10 Divisions
		Submarine Units		2 Divisions	4 Divisions	6 Divisions
		Minesweeping Units	1 Flotilla	2 Flotillas	2 Flotillas	2 Flotillas
		Land-Based Anti-Submarine Aircraft Units	9 Squadrons	15 Squadrons	14 Squadrons	16 Squadrons
	Major equipment	Anti-Submarine Surface Ships	57 Ships	59 Ships	59 Ships	61 Ships
		Submarines	2 Submarines	7 Submarines	12 Submarines	14 Submarines
		Operational Aircraft	(Apx. 220 Aircraft)	(Apx. 230 Aircraft)	(Apx. 240 Aircraft)	Apx. 210 Aircraft (Apx. 300 Aircraft)
ASDF	**Basic Units**	Aircraft Control and Warning Units	24 Groups	24 Groups	24 Groups	28 Groups
		Interceptor Units	12 Squadrons	15 Squadrons	10 Squadrons	10 Squadrons
		Support Fighter Units		4 Squadrons	4 Squadrons	3 Squadrons
		Air Reconnaissance Units		1 Squadron	1 Squadron	1 Squadron
		Air Transport Units	2 Squadrons	3 Squadrons	3 Squadrons	3 Squadrons
		Early Warning Units				
		High-Altitude Ground-to-Air Missile Units		2 Groups	4 Groups	5 Groups (Another group being prepared)
	Major equipment	Operational Aircraft	(Apx. 1,130 Aircraft)	(Apx. 1,100 Aircraft)	(Apx. 940 Aircraft)	Apx. 490 Aircraft (Apx. 900 Aircraft)

Note: Parenthesized numbers of operational aircraft denote total number of aircraft including trainers. The numbers of units from the 1st to 3rd Buildup Plans are as of the end of each plan period.

rather than about the existence of the SDFs. On the one hand, it seemed to LDP leaders in times of trouble that further buildup of the SDFs would give the opposition the ammunition it was looking for. On the other hand, if the government would promise to forgo further arms buildups by putting a ceiling on SDF strength, the opposition might be persuaded to live with the status quo in national defense as a trade-off. In short, the government needed to appease the opposition with a compromise. When the idea was broached to the Defense bureaucracy, it struck one official as the "worst joke" he had ever heard.

As government power passed to Tanaka, the idea of freezing the SDFs firmed up and was reinforced by additional incentives. When Tanaka went to Peking shortly after Nixon's trip, to normalize Japan–China relations he received Chou En-lai's assurance that China would no longer attack Japan's security arrangements. The loss of Chinese support isolated Japan's Socialists.

Then in 1973 the Arab oil embargo and price hike came. The attendant inflationary impact was multiplied by the mistaken fiscal policy of the Tanaka cabinet. Skyrocketing costs all but stalled arms acquisition midway through the fourth defense buildup plan. In the era of stable, or zero, growth that followed, the defense budget could not be increased, and Prime Minister Miki canonized "1 percent of GNP" as an uncrossable barrier.

It fell to Kubo Takuya, the administrative vice minister of defense under the Miki cabinet, and other officials to work out a defense posture that conformed to the political strategy of the LDP. Theirs was an impossible task; they had to provide for the country's external defense and at the same time satisfy the pacifist opposition within. Perforce they had to ignore any external threat that might cost more than what Japan could pay for within 1 percent of GNP. Thus Kubo came up with the standard defense force concept [*kiban-teki bōei-ryoku kōsō*] and the transcending-the-threat thesis [*datsu kyōi ron*] to defend it.[18] Kubo might as well have called the latter the ignoring-the-threat thesis.

What purposes the SDFs can serve when they "ignore" any threat costing more than 1 percent of GNP was left vague by Kubo. He seemed to imply that the SDFs can meet Japan's "international responsibility." Under the present circumstances, this can only mean "responsibility" to the United States, for whatever Japan cannot or will not do by way of external defense falls on the shoulders of the American ally, who must also be politically appeased. In this sense, Japan's defense establishment may be regarded not as an insurance policy but as a premium paid on one.

Under the standard defense force concept (more accurately, the nucleus or foundational defense force concept), Japan would let the capabilities of the SDFs fall "far short" of the stated goal of past buildup plans, that is, to meet localized aggression by conventional means. Instead the concept sets forth a goal that is "specific" and "attainable": to build a peacetime defense force adequate to cope with "limited and small-scale aggression." At the same time, however, this force is assumed to be an adequate *nucleus* or *foundation* for "smooth" further buildups "when serious changes in the situation demand" them.[19] In other words, the standard defense force is assumed to be an adequate screen behind which the country can mobilize if a threat greater than "limited and small-scale aggression" is encountered. In that event, the standard defense force will also enable Japan to fight a holding action until American reaction forces arrive and join with Japanese forces to expel the invader. The standard defense force serves these three purposes—at least formally. A defense posture that avowedly ignores external threat until it materializes is what I prefer to call the posture of "waiting for a Pearl Harbor."

One may ask how a scaled-down capability can be assumed to be an adequate nucleus for emergency expansion. According to the 1978 Defense White Paper, "the 'National Defense Program Outline' does not simply estimate quantities of defense 'capability' in light of potential threats."[20] Instead it assumes that the *intentions* of Japan's neighbors are more relevant to her defense planning than are their capabilities. Japan has thus abandoned the past practice of trying to maintain some proportion between her own defense capability and the capability of potential enemies because this practice is politically and fiscally unattainable.

Both the 1977 and 1978 Defense White Papers offer elaborate analyses of the international situation surrounding Japan since the beginning of détente. They stress the general reduction in international tension as the hallmark of the new situation. In this assessment, the White Papers closely parallel the 1979 posture statement by U.S. Secretary of Defense Harold Brown.[21] Formally at least, the standard defense force concept is presented as an adjustment to the new situation. In the sense that the concept rests on justification of Japan's defense posture through strategic analysis, it looks like an improvement over past buildup plans, which tended to be more or less simple weapons acquisition programs without doctrinal foundations.

Specifically, Outline is based on the following assumptions about Japan's international environment:

1) The Japan-U.S. security system will be effectively maintained in the future.

2) The United States and the Soviet Union will continue to avert nuclear warfare or large-scale conflict which could develop into nuclear warfare.

3) Sino-Soviet confrontation will continue even if partial improvements in their relations are seen.

4) The United States and China will move to adjust their relations in the future.

5) The status quo will be maintained on the Korean Peninsula, and no large-scale armed conflict will break out.[22]

Formally, the premise of the standard defense force concept is that "there will be no serious changes in this environment." If this premise becomes untenable, Japan will scramble to increase its readiness.

During the 1978 controversy, the main criticism against General Kurisu amounted to this: Where is the threat that would justify an instantaneous local reaction? Kurisu's critics maintained—not without plausibility—that any military threat to a country is always preceded by a protracted period of tension, allowing ample time for necessary mobilization. But this argument misses the point: the standard defense force concept is an adjustment not to the new international situation but to the 1 percent of GNP ceiling, a strictly domestic political requirement.

To put it bluntly, the standard defense force concept assumes that Japan's neighbors do not harbor hostile *intentions* toward her. If this assumption were pushed to its logical conclusion, the need for a peacetime military establishment would disappear. In one sense, however, the concept does take into account the *capabilities* of potential enemies. According to Outline, "Japan will repel limited and small-scale aggression in principle without external assistance." Since the capability required for this mission would be maintained regardless of the intentions of Japan's neighbors, such capability is presumably geared to that of a potential enemy. This is the upper limit of the operational, as opposed to the deterrent, function of the SDFs.

Moreover, Japan does take into account the capabilities of her potentially hostile neighbors in one other respect: the quality of arms. The standard defense force concept dictates the possession and maintenance of at least one of each variety of tactical unit that meets the highest international standard and can be expanded in cases of need.

Suppose we conceive of an ascending scale of conflicts as follows:

1) indirect aggression or inciting rebellion;

2) use or threat to use force short of war;

3) limited and small-scale invasion;
4) limited war (the Korean War, for instance);
5) total conventional war;
6) nuclear war.

Between the second and the fourth defense buildup plans, the SDFs were formally assigned the mission of coping with conflicts 1) through 4). The 1976 Outline has lowered the SDF sight by one notch to conflict 3). Correspondingly, the range of contingencies that call for American military assistance has been broadened from conflicts 5) and 6) to conflicts 4) through 6).

If an invasion involved a conflict ranging in scale from 4) through 6), Japan would offer "an unyielding resistance by mobilizing all available forces until such times as cooperation from the United States is introduced," says Outline. This constitutes the deterrent function of the standard defense force and the Japan-U.S. security system.

Having lowered their sights to attainable goals, the Defense Agency was able to lay down for the first time rather specific levels of arms maintenance, replacement schedules, and accompanying budgets. Roughly speaking, the level of "forward defense capability" (front-line military hardware) acquired by the end of the fourth defense buildup plan will be maintained, and the efforts of the SDFs under Outline will extend to improving logistic and rear services, survivability of military installations, command/control/communication functions, and, above all, surveillance functions to detect changes in the intentions of Japan's neighbors.

What Japan may decide to do once its survival is threatened is difficult to predict. But Outline seems to be saying this to the country: "What with the Three Principles of Nuclear Disarmament, the ban on dispatch of troops abroad, the '1 percent of GNP' ceiling, and so on, the range of ends the nation can hope to pursue is limited. If you want to be secure against other contingencies, you will have to pay correspondingly more. Japan is running risks. But the responsibilities lie not with defense planners but with the country."

The responsibilities in question do not simply mean fixing the blame for failure. They presumably include proper statecraft or diplomacy to steer the country clear of military conflicts. To define national security as military plus nonmilitary elements is so self-evident as to be a platitude. To those who stress "defense plus" in Japan, however, it seems to be a synonym for "less for defense." (Ōhira took this stance while he was running for the LDP presidency but reversed himself once he won.) They have yet to answer this query: Is diplomacy able to avert any and all military conflicts without presupposing ultimate Finlandization? But security consciousness as a motivation for defense may not solve Japan's problem; she may have to develop a sense of honor before she can meet her security needs, because national honor is ultimately the only effective counter to those who assume "better red than dead" on grounds of security alone.

Taken as a declaratory strategy, the standard defense force concept defeats its own purpose by transcending external threat, that is, by admitting openly that Japan is not serious about defense. In rationalizing away external threat to preserve Japan's pacifism, it comes close to being an "opiate of the masses." The real purpose of the concept was to compel the radical-liberal opposition to accept the existence of the SDFs. In that sense the concept must receive double credit, for to accept the limited role of the SDFs is also to accept an almost unlimited American role to make up for the SDFs shortfalls. To recognize the SDFs as a slow trip wire would be meaningless unless there is a big bang at the end of it. Perhaps it was for this reason that U.S. Defense Secretary Brown was laudatory in 1979 of Japan's new defense posture. But America's joy of being taken seriously as an ally for the first time is bound to be ephemeral. When that joy gives way to anger at Japan's alleged free ride, the standard defense force concept makes Japan vulnerable to unreasonable American pressure.

In strict dollar terms, Japan's 1978 defense budget of $9.6 billion compares not too unfavorably with Britain's $13.6 billion or France's $17.5 billion. But the standard defense force concept concedes that Japan's outlay serves not so much national defense as an ulterior purpose of securing American protection. Instead of reserving to Japan the right to determine the nature of external threat and appropriate countermeasures, the concept surrenders that right to the United States along with an additional privilege to name a price for the protection. The United States may underperform its role as a protector; she may become overzealous; or she may ask for what she regards as a "fair return" in areas unrelated to defense. For instance, there is a tendency for Japan's security to implicitly become a hostage in trade disputes because recently the United States is in the habit of getting economic concessions tacitly understood as compensation for being the protector. This tendency will be the greater, the more the American people perceive the alliance as a favor to Japan. And the point here is that the standard defense force concept encourages and amplifies that perception.

Fortunately, however, the standard defense concept is a transitional device geared to a passing phase in early 1970s when Japanese public was still pacifist but increasingly pro-American. When that pacifism evaporates, it will become possible for defense planners to return to the more orthodox practice of establishing a formal link between the perception of threat and defense capability.

When measured in terms of the unstated political goal of legitimizing the SDFs, the accomplishment of the new defense posture is not inconsiderable. The SDFs have been a "ghetto" army in the past; its personnel would remove their uniforms upon leaving the camps to avoid public disdain. The demoralization of troops was reflected in the inability of the SDFs to perform the few missions that were assigned them. Airmen were not allowed to have airspace for training; troops in Okinawa could not hold firing practice because of local opposition; the ammunition store was allowed to be depleted to a ridiculously low level; logistic and rear services were in a sad state; the command/control /communication function was so neglected that when a pilot flying a MIG-25 sought asylum in 1976, the Joint Staff Council was not aware of the incident for several hours; fixed radar sites atop mountains were completely unguarded and exposed; elementary security measures around military installations were disregarded; there were virtually no reserve forces to back up the regulars; and so on and on. These conditions will change. Japan's SDFs will count in what little they are supposed to do.

A few words are in order here on the composition of forces and tactical units envisioned by Outline (see Table 3). The ground SDF is authorized to have 180,000 personnel (actually filled to 86 percent of authorization) in an equivalent of thirteen divisions. Understrength divisions save on personnel costs, which accounted for 54.4 percent of the defense budget in 1978. In the past, ground SDF units were dispersed rather evenly across Japan, allegedly for the purpose of maintaining domestic order. This is questionable, especially if the strength of the ground SDF needs to be increased, as its chief of staff stated in March 1979, to cope with the Soviet buildup in the Northern Territories (only a stone's throw away from Hokkaido) claimed by Japan but occupied by the Soviet Union since 1945. The days when Japan was split over the alliance with the United States are gone, and domestic security should be relegated to a lower order of priority for the ground SDF. The SDFs should first concentrate their strength in the north, the south, and the center, in that order, before asking for an increase in strength. I welcome the latest decision of the Defense Agency to favor troop concentration in the north.

The Maritime SDF had originally hoped to acquire five escort groups (of eight destroyers each) in order to keep two groups in a state of high alert—presumably one each for the Pacific and the Sea of Japan. But because more than half of its vessels now in use are due to be retired in the next ten

TABLE 3
Standard Defense Force

			Authorized number of SDF personnel	180,000 persons
GSDF	Basic units		Units deployed regionally in peacetime	12 Divisions 2 Composite Brigades
			Mobile Operation Units	1 Armored Division 1 Artillery Brigade 1 Airborne Brigade 1 Training Brigade 1 Helicopter Brigade
			Low-Altitude Ground-to-Air Missile Units	8 Anti-Aircraft Artillery Groups
MSDF	Basic units		Anti-Submarine Surface-Ship Units (for mobile operation)	4 Escort Flotillas
			Anti-Submarine Surface-Ship Units (Regional District Units)	10 Divisions
			Submarine Units	6 Divisions
			Minesweeping Units	2 Flotillas
			Land-Based Anti-Submarine Aircraft Units	16 Squadrons
	Main equipment		Anti-Submarine Surface Ships	Approx. 60 Ships
			Submarines	16 Submarines
			Operational Aircraft	Approx. 220 Aircraft
ASDF	Basic units		Aircraft Control and Warning Units	28 Groups
			Interceptor Units	10 Squadrons
			Support Fighter Units	3 Squadrons
			Air Reconnaissance Units	1 Squadron
			Air Transport Units	3 Squadrons
			Early Warning Units	1 Squadron
			High-Altitude Ground-to-Air Missile Units	6 Groups
	Main equipment		Operational Aircraft	Approx. 430 Aircraft

Note: This list is based upon the equipment structure that the SDF possesses, or is scheduled to possess, at the time of the drafting of this National Defense Program Outline.

years, the Maritime SDF could ask for only four escort groups in order to have one in readiness at all times.

One escort group of eight destroyers to protect Japan! This means that the stated goal of Outline to protect only Japan's home waters comes down to a choice between the Pacific and the Japan Sea.

Sixteen submarines, instead of the eighteen originally requested, will be stationed at the Sōya, Tsushima, and Tsugaru straits. Of the 220 aircraft of the Maritime SDF, somewhere between 150 and 170 will take up anti-submarine warfare functions. The Maritime SDF will also acquire twelve Lock-heed C-130 Hercules transport aircraft shortly for mine-laying and strait-blockading purposes. Transports will be outfitted for this purpose because bombers are said to be unconstitutional.

The Maritime SDF, whose acquisition of Lockheed P3Cs for anti-sub-marine warfare was delayed because of the scandal, will at long last get the first 8 in late 1979—to be followed by 37 more for a total of 45. They will be part of a force of about 170 aircraft of various types to take up the anti-sub-marine mission.

Authorization was also granted in 1979 for the purchase of four Grumman E2Cs by 1983 for the purpose of providing airborne early warning (look-down) surveillance. This is an attempt to remedy the inability of existing radars (in 28 sites) to detect low-flying intrusions into Japan's airspace as demonstrated by the MIG-25 incident of 1976. The Defense Agency plans to acquire a total of eight E2Cs, and to organize two reconnaissance squadrons in time. This is hardly enough, of course. To provide an around-the-clock surveillance over Japan, some twenty E2Cs each for a minimum of seven air watch stations are said to be necessary. The first four E2Cs, therefore, will serve the training and trial purposes for the time being.

For intercepting intruders into Japan's airspace, the air SDF will need thirteen to fifteen squadrons at six or seven airbases around the country. Outline proposes to maintain the current ten interceptor squadrons and three ground-support squadrons—the latter doubling as interceptors—for this purpose. The three ground-support squadrons will use the Japanese-devel-oped F-1 fighters, while the interceptor squadrons will be equipped with F-4 Phantoms and F-15 Eagles, of which 100 will be purchased over time. Unlike the Phantoms, the F-15s will keep their air-refueling equipment.

A 1979 cabinet decision renewed the injunction that defense spending is not to exceed 1 percent of GNP "for the time being." The Defense budget for 1978 came to 0.9 percent of GNP, or ¥1,900 billion (a little under $10 billion). The budget for fiscal 1979 was ¥2,134 billion, or well in excess of $10 billion, making it the seventh largest in the world. This included an increase of some $70 million (to total $750 million) in cost sharing for U.S. forces in Japan (the U.S. share was $1.1 billion).

The Defense Agency is drawing up what amounts to the fifth defense buildup plan (for 1980–1984) with a total budget of ¥12,000 billion, or about $60 billion. This figure excludes outlays for base facilities. Under the fifth plan, the agency seeks to improve the Base Air Defense Ground Environment (BADGE) system in order to integrate the F-15s and E2Cs (air early warning aircraft) into the air defense command; purchase new ground-to-air missiles to replace the obsolete NIKEs; and reorganize and revamp the Ground SDF divisions for the first time in twenty years for the specific purposes of matching Soviet improvements in motorization, increased firepower, and helicopter-borne mobility.

NATO-TYPE MILITARY INTEGRATION

Outline goes hand in glove with Guideline. But the timing for making Guideline public—at the end of the 1978 controversy—suggests that the Japanese government wanted to gauge public reaction to its own defense posture before revealing its implications for the alliance. Having disavowed unattainable goals in building defense capabilities, Japan has agreed in Guideline to cooperate much more closely with U.S. armed forces. In a sense, Guideline represents the dream of the U.S. Defense Department come true; it presages close strategic and tactical cooperation of American and Japanese forces in the defense not only of Japan but of the Far East as well. In spite of the proviso that the two national forces are not to submit to a common command, Guideline points to de facto NATO-type cooperation. In this sense, Guideline represents a new departure in the alliance, though this point is played down.

In Guideline, the two national forces agreed to conduct studies on joint defense planning; undertake joint exercises and training; prepare beforehand common operational procedures, including intelligence, logistics, and communications/electronics; establish coordinated common readiness stages; and maintain a coordination center.

On the modalities of common defense operations against aggression, Guideline determines the division of labor between the two national forces. The United States promises to maintain nuclear arms for the purpose of deterrence and to undertake forward deployment of fast reaction forces in the event of attack. Japan, for its part, will make the initial denial and holding action until American succor arrives; then the two forces will launch a joint counteroffensive. The assigned missions of the two forces are complementary, with the U.S. forces exercising strategic functions. This is the natural consequence of the self-imposed restriction on the Japanese forces to operate in their home territory, water, and airspace.

On the question of coping with threats to areas of the Far East other than Japan, Guideline is cautiously closemouthed. It simply requires the two countries to consult on changes in the international situation. In addition,

Japan has agreed to offer additional base facilities to the U.S. forces if necessary.

Two contradictory assessments of Guideline and its implications can be made. On the one hand, given the extent of integration and coordination between the two national forces spelled out in Guideline, the subordination of the SDFs to U.S. armed forces in wartime, if not in peace, is inescapable for two reasons. First, the United States will carry out strategic functions while Japan confines itself to more tactical ones. Second, because of cultural, linguistic, and historical factors, the SDFs will defer to U.S. forces at all levels. Arguably, the subordination of Japanese to U.S. forces would not matter if Japan retained autonomy in strategic decisions to deploy the entire allied force.

But this argument seems to be of doubtful value. War is notorious for having its own momentum, and for Japan to pretend that she has the power to veto strategic operations undertaken by the United States, especially if Japan does not take part in them, would be fatuous. War conducted on the basis of Guideline will surely expose the alleged mutuality of the Japan-U.S. Security Treaty for what it is: a myth. The inequality between the two allied powers has been a source of concern among radical-liberals and conservatives throughout the postwar years. Here we are touching on the most basic and intractable issue in the alliance.

On the other hand, Guideline can be regarded as an excellent document that should have been drawn up long ago. Since Japan is unwilling to be self-reliant in matters of defense, she should be only too grateful that the United States will and can protect her. If the United States prefers a NATO-type coordination with Japanese forces, Japan's accession to that preference can be regarded as additional insurance strengthening the alliance.

But there is another, more important reason for welcoming Guideline. Japan's defense posture is one of "waiting for a Pearl Harbor." Presumably the more advance planning and preparations there are, the softer will be Japan's landing on the morrow of a "Pearl Harbor." Knowing that Japan will have to mobilize under politically risky conditions, the United States would be well advised to be aboveboard in strategic decisions and planning. Having a carefully prepared procedure to govern cooperation between the two countries will be of great help in insuring open communication.

Against the backdrop of the Soviet aircraft carrier *Minsk* steaming past the Japanese archipelago, along with creeping uncertainty in allied leadership in Washington, phase two of the defense controversy is taking place. Buoyed by the dissipation of anti-American and antimilitary sentiments, the uniformed officers of the Defense Agency stand in the forefront of the assault on Japan's bankrupt defense posture.

Some of the more noteworthy developments in 1979 included announcement by the three uniformed services of long-delayed plans to conduct joint exercises with their U.S. counterparts; revelation by the Defense Agency of what amounts to the fifth defense buildup plan (which will spend up to 1 percent of GNP rather than 0.9 percent as at present), in spite of the earlier understanding that the fourth plan was to be the last; the historic first visit by Defense Minister Yamashita to the Republic of Korea, which symbolized Japan's interest in regional security; Yamashita's subsequent public acknowledgment in Washington that the increased Soviet presence in Asia is a "threat" to Japan; and publication of the 1979 Defense White Paper (July), which upgraded the Soviet threat so as to pave the way for a revision of the standard defense force concept.

These developments are taking place in the context of broader debate about the nature and orientation of pacifist Japan. They are fueled by the latest wave of American and West European criticism of Japan's "free ride." Many Japanese are as exasperated as their foreign detractors about their government's lack of initiative.

Will all this mean that Japan will shortly discard the posture of transcending external threat, or of "waiting for a Pearl Harbor" to confront it? One can reasonably expect the LDP government to increase the defense budget incrementally beyond 1 percent of GNP over the next several years. But that leaves intact the most crucial constitutional barrier: defensive defense. If the standard defense force concept is revised, another equally unsatisfactory arrangement may have to replace it because it is the constitution itself that prevents Japan from fully translating a perceived threat into corresponding military preparedness.

CHAPTER FOUR

Scramble for Survival

It is the policy of the Japanese government to 1) meet limited and small-scale aggression by its own efforts; and 2) to meet larger threats with a mobilization of its resources after the fact and 3) in alliance with the United States. The test of Japan's defense posture is whether it can accomplish these three goals.

Japan's strategic concern focuses on three areas of the world: the Soviet Far East, North Korea, and the Middle East. Thus, Japan underwrote President Carter's recent peace efforts in the Middle East by offering large-scale aid to Egypt. But presumably, no matter how much Japan mobilizes under threat, her defense concern will not extend beyond East Asia and the western Pacific. Outline makes no mention of peace in the Middle East as a premise of the standard defense force concept. Japan will not mobilize even if a regional conflict arises in the Middle East, according to current government policy.

This reflects the U.S. defense posture, to which Japan's defense posture is logically linked. The defense posture of the United States is based on the assumption that she will not have to fight more than one and a half wars simultaneously. Consequently, the United States will have to choose between the Middle East and Korea as theaters for waging its half war. The United States takes for granted that a conflict in the Middle East that involves the United States and forces her to vacate her troops elsewhere will not create instability in East Asia. This is a dangerous assumption, both for Japan and for the United States.

The defense posture that envisions fighting one and a half wars is justified on the ground that the Sino-Soviet tension compels the two countries to tie down considerable parts of their armies along the common border. Sino-American détente, in addition, is thought to give the United States the leverage to manipulate this tension to the advantage of the West. Secondarily, the miraculous surge of South Korean economic strength combined with stagnation in North Korea is said to reduce the chance that Pyongyang will be tempted to invade South Korea.

There is no gainsaying the facts that Sino-Soviet tension exists or that it is beneficial to the West. Neither the tension nor China's opening to the West, however, makes her an ally of Japan or NATO. China is an adventurous and mischievous power, as her invasion of Vietnam in 1979 indicates. Her détente with the United States and Japan is based not on any shared values, but solely on a calculation of her interests. Presumably the Chinese calculate that the strong presence of American power in East Asia augments China's as yet relatively weak power vis-à-vis the Soviets. What China, a fair-weather friend of the West, would do if the U.S. presence in East Asia were reduced is difficult to predict. But it would be utter folly to assume that China would take on the role of deputy sheriff of the United States while the sheriff is off from East Asia on a posse. The temptation for China to make mischief will be all the greater if the international situation becomes more fluid. Thus, she may liberate Taiwan—just as Stalin annexed a part of Poland—on the assumption that the West will acquiesce in a fait accompli. We must remember that until recently the Chinese Communist party's official doctrine anticipated a conflict between the United States and the Soviet Union (the tiger and the wolf) and predicted that China would make some obliquely hinted gains.

Soon after the conclusion of the Sino-Japanese peace treaty and Washington's recognition of Peking, Japan's foreign minister, Sonoda, initiated a move to remove Taiwan from the list of the mutual concerns of Japan and the United States under the Far Eastern clause of the Security Treaty but was rebuffed by the United States. What this means is not clear. Neither is the American intention toward Taiwan. Washington may have wished to wait until the formal lapse of its mutual security treaty with the Nationalist Chinese government in 1980 before removing Taiwan from the mutual concern classification under the Japan-U.S. Security Treaty. On the other hand, moves in the U.S. Congress suggest that Washington wishes to retain some influence over Taiwan's security indefinitely. This is welcome from Japan's standpoint. Japan's acts as a pacifist commercial democracy are not necessarily in her best strategic interests. That is, she may agree to abandon Taiwan formally and even take the initiative in pushing her drowning quondam friend under, but Japan's confidence in her alliance with the United States may nonetheless be shaken if Taiwan is forcibly "liberated." This is one dastardly aspect of Japan as a pacifist state that the United States should remember. The only solution to this problem is to change the Japanese regime.

Only the Soviet Union can pose the threat of invading Japan proper. The "small-scale and limited aggression" that Outline contemplates is an isolated surprise attack that may be tempting to the Soviet Union if Japan is defenseless. The standard defense force seems adequate to repel such an invasion. It raises the threshold of invasion by raising the cost to the Soviets of undertaking such an attack. Even in the absence of the Japan-U.S. Security Treaty, it is doubtful that the Soviets could launch an invasion of Japan with total immunity from American reaction. Hence it is doubtful that they would do so except as part of a global conflict. In such a conflict between the NATO and Warsaw Pact powers, the Soviets would have a vital interest in deploying their strategic nuclear striking force. To secure the right of passage from Vladivostok to the Pacific for her Far Eastern fleet, she might occupy the northern part of Hokkaido that fronts on the Sōya Strait. The recent buildup of the Soviet garrison in Japan's occupied Northern Territories is said to have been for this purpose.

In a global war the Soviets might also preempt Japan's decision for war or peace through indiscriminate sinking of allied merchant shipping. But Japan has one rather potent point of leverage over the Soviet Union: her ability to bottle up the Soviet navy in the Japan Sea. This might cause the Soviets to bargain with Japan. By promising to exempt Japanese merchant shipping from attacks and thus sparing Japan involvement in a world conflict, the Soviets might ask for free passage to the Pacific. While the Soviet Union is engaged with NATO, she would have a strong incentive not to open a second front with China. China might make a lot of noise, but her interests, too, would be to keep the peace with the Soviets; she will watch the tiger and the wolf fight each other. Japan might be inclined to side with China and remain neutral. The Soviet Union could reinforce such an inclination, not only with threats against Japan's merchant shipping, but with nuclear blackmail against major Japanese cities. Protesting her innocence, Japan might in effect slip out of allied war efforts. She would then resemble Kuomintang China in the latter half of the Second World War, when it was nominally an Allied power but was in fact neutral vis-à-vis Japan.

Or, the United States might preempt Japan's entry into the war by using the Seventh Fleet and air force units in Japan, Korea, and Okinawa to launch an air assault on Soviet naval and air bases at the outset of war. Such an act could create an enormous strain in the Japan-U.S. alliance. The United States would be under a strong moral obligation to fulfill its guarantee of Japan's security, including nuclear deterrence. Nevertheless, the Soviet Union might call America's bluff by launching a limited nuclear assault on Japan for the specific purpose of testing America's resolve to protect Japan. If the United States wavered, Japan would pay dearly for having built herself up as a "half power."

It is quite possible that NATO's just war with the Soviet Union could touch off a ground swell of sympathy among the Japanese for the United States, much as the French Revolution did among the American people. But on the other hand, Japan has legitimate grounds for doubting whether in a crisis originating on the NATO front or in the Middle East the United States will protect Japan as it will protect Western Europe. This is especially true with respect to the protection of Japan's merchant fleet against commerce-raiding submarines. Secretary of Defense Brown exudes confidence on this point in his 1979 Report to the Congress: ". . . our forces could quickly reduce any overseas bases they [the Soviets] might have at the outset of the campaign . . . it could take as many as three months to bring the Soviet submarine threat under control in the Atlantic and the Pacific." But his optimism is at variance both with the judgments of other authorities and, above all, with the actual decline of U.S. naval power.

A cost-effectiveness study of strategic alternatives by the U.S. Congressional Budget Office in 1977 drew a clear line at the Persian Gulf and distinguished what lies to the east of it from what is to the west. The mission of the U.S. Navy in the Atlantic, according to the study, is to protect allied reaction forces from Soviet attack, but in the Pacific only the Japanese merchant marine calls for protection. The study notes, quite correctly, that Japan is virtually the only beneficiary of the U.S. Navy's attempt to keep open the sea-lane from the Persian Gulf through the Indian Ocean and the Malacca Strait. A Brookings Institution study of 1977 de-emphasizes the geopolitical importance of the Pacific as a theater of contention with the Soviet Union and recommends a gradual move away from two-ocean deployment.[23] Admiral Holloway, chief of naval operations, in testimony before the House Armed Services Committee in 1977, also stated that the U.S. Navy will have its hands full in keeping open the sea-lanes from the west coast to Hawaii and Alaska, and that it will find patrolling the western Pacific difficult. One can go on citing many other statements that contradict Defense Secretary Brown. But this much can be concluded safely: the chief mission of the U.S. Navy, as indeed that of the Soviet Far East fleet, is offensive, not defensive, in nature; escorting merchant shipping in the Pacific is low on the list of U.S. priorities.

An overt and large-scale East-West conflict preceded by sufficient warning offers one advantage to Japan. If handled skillfully, the shock will be a catalyst for rapid mobilization; it will be a "Pearl Harbor." However, the Soviet naval threat may come in a more diffuse form that falls short of open hostility. The Soviet Navy may continue rising relative to the U.S. Navy; it now uses bases in Camranh Bay and may acquire additional bases elsewhere.

Eventually the Soviet Union may reach a point where she can use her superior force for the purpose of political blackmail. Such a diffuse threat will be the most difficult one for pacifist Japan to handle, as it may divide the public. A slowly rising diffuse threat could persuade the pacifists that doing nothing is the better part of wisdom. If that were to happen, pacifism would become self-reinforcing.

The Maritime SDF was consciously designed to be a supporting arm of the U.S. Navy; anti-submarine warfare in Japan's home waters to provide cover for offensive ships of the U.S. Navy nearly exhausts its functions. Japan's arsenal includes few missile-firing ships. Her anti-submarine capability consists of 150 to 170 aircraft and 32 destroyers in four flotillas, of which only one flotilla is to be kept at the state of high alert. That means 8 destroyers! Japan is obviously not serious about anti-submarine warfare in her home waters, nor is she serious about protecting the sea-line of communication for overseas commerce. It is also evident that 32 destroyers and their crews are inadequate as a standard defense force, that is, as a nucleus for further expansion in times of need. There are two problems here: quantitative and qualitative. Japan could conceivably increase the size of her destroyer fleet three-fold or fourfold within the limits of the standard defense force. But to project the fleet's anti-submarine warfare capability abroad would presuppose a change in the character of the Japanese state—although as a commercial regime, Japan is more dependent on overseas commerce than any other country in the world.

All the more surprising is the Maritime SDF's apparent seriousness about the operation to seal off the Soviet navy's exits to the Pacific. But the will to use this weapon may be lost if Japan is vulnerable in every other respect.

All the same, Japan must plan to meet and survive a possible crisis. The Air SDF must increase the size of its fighter-interceptor force and provide for its protection on the ground. The beginning of air early warning surveillance is welcome and should be strengthened.

In the past few years, a rather broad-based discussion of the concept of a pan-Pacific community has been under way in Japan. The concept includes the rimland of the Asian continent but excludes China. It suggests a political, economic, and cultural union of noncommunist states in the region, and as such it is meant to be an alternative to continentalism for Japan. Prime Minister Ōhira is personally interested in the movement. Japan's defense planners should study the strategic implications of the concept as a possible fallback against the Soviet naval threat and disruption of the oil supply from the Persian Gulf. Japan must seriously study the possibility of forgoing the sea-line of communication east of the Malacca Strait and trying to survive instead by importing the basic minimum from friends and allies in the Pacific basin, including Australia, Canada, Indonesia, Mexico, and the United States. Combined with increased stockpiling of critical materials (a 90-day supply for oil at present), this strategy could enable Japan to survive for one year.

We have grounds for greater optimism when we come to the Korean question. In March 1979 the Carter administration decided to hold in abeyance its unwise policy of withdrawing ground combat units and nuclear weapons from the Korean peninsula. The Carter administration and Congress have stopped their attempt to shake up the government of South Korea with Koreagate and human rights issues. All those who are concerned about the stability of East Asia welcome the new turn in Washington. We are not asking America to ignore ethics in politics; we merely ask that she be more prudent. After all, who could say that the United States has not lent a helping hand to the revolutionaries in Iran by raising the human rights issue against the shah? Following his fall and U.S. derecognition of Taiwan, the Korean withdrawal probably could not have gone on without creating a falling domino psychology in Asia. Already Korean-Japanese economic ties have grown since 1977 to brace for the announced U.S. retreat.

The Republic of Korea has replaced Japan as the miracle of Asia since the onset of the worldwide recession created by the oil price hikes. This surge in South Korea was motivated by the strategic decision to increase her self-reliance after the Carter administration's announcement of withdrawal. But enforced development under a dictatorship apparently exacted a toll by creating a strain in South Korea's political system, and the strain erupted in the assassination of President Park Chung Hee. Thanks to the swift warning by the United States against outside interference, however, there was no immediate harm to the Korean peninsula's stability. It is hoped that South Korea will use this opportunity to shift toward a more benign and viable government. China's opening to the West and the triangular relationship among Peking, Washington, and Moscow have created a situation in which neither Peking nor Moscow seems interested in encouraging Kim Il-song's adventurous impulse. With the U.S. ground combat forces staying on, one can trust Defense Secretary Brown's view that "the North Koreans could not be assured of achieving decisive results in the initial days of their offensive."[24] Against an *isolated and local* conflict in the peninsula, therefore, Japan can count on a minimum screen behind which to mobilize beyond the standard defense force level.

The Japanese people are slowly coming to realize that the days when they could stand idly by while Americans died defending Korea will never return. Partly because of Korea's significance in the anti-Soviet balance, the United States will honor its commitment to perform a deterrent function there. But if deterrence fails, the political situation in the United States will be such as to require that "Japanese boys" fight alongside and even replace "American boys." This cannot be otherwise, in my judgment. The future defense of South Korea must be based on tripartite cooperation that includes dispatching Japanese combat troops. At present it is politically unfeasible for the Japanese government to make such a war plan, and it would be foolhardy to jeopardize the still fragile consensus on defense with a premature challenge to the constitutional bans. But nonmilitary cooperation between Japan and South Korea must be maintained at the highest degree possible.

A gnawing sense of doubt is spreading in Japan about the U.S. will to honor its commitments to defend East Asia. Japan would rather not speak of it for fear of damaging America's credibility, because as things stand today Japan has no recourse other than alliance with the United States. Japan simply must assume that the full panoply of American arsenals will be forthcoming for her defense. For reasons suggested in chapter one, Japan's willingness to honor her obligation toward the alliance is the strongest it has ever been. Because of the importance of the alliance not only for Japan's defense but also for international trade, Japan can and should be induced to do more on two fronts: she should eliminate the trade surplus with the United States to minimize friction; she should do more within the existing defense posture for her own defense.

But ultimately the United States must ask the following questions of herself and come up with answers:

—Is the alliance with Japan worthwhile?

—If so, but if the cost is unbearable, should the alliance continue in the present form?

—What are the purposes of the alliance with Japan? One of the original purposes was to keep a tight leash on Japan so as to forestall any chance of resurgent militarism. Is such a fear still warranted today?

In conclusion I return once again to the title of this book: *Waiting for a Pearl Harbor*. Someday a security crisis is going to knock on Japan's door. One of two things will follow: Japan will fail to overcome the crisis, in which case her pacifism will confirm itself; or she will meet the crisis successfully and in doing so will shed her pacifism.

Perhaps all successful democracies are pacifist commercial democracies to some degree. America was such a country on the eves of its war of independence and of Pearl Harbor. Yet, as Alexis de Tocqueville observed:

> When serious dangers threaten the state, the people frequently succeed in selecting the citizens who are the most able to save it. It has been observed that man rarely retains his customary level in very critical circumstances; he rises above or sinks below his usual condition, and the same thing is true of nations. Extreme perils sometimes quench the energy of a people instead of stimulating it; they excite without directing its passions; and instead of clearing they confuse its powers of perception. The Jews fought and killed one another amid the smoking ruins of their temple. But it is more common, with both nations and individuals, to find extraordinary virtues developed from the very imminence of the danger. Great characters are then brought into relief as the edifices which are usually concealed by the gloom of night are illuminated by the glare of a conflagration. At those dangerous times genius no longer hesitates to come forward; and the people, alarmed by the perils of their situation, for a time forget their envious passions. Great names may then be drawn from the ballot box.[25]

Somewhere along the path that Japan is to take in the future lurks the chance that will allow her to rise above and discard her pacifist past.

CHAPTER FIVE

Looking to the Future

Japan did not spend herself in World War II. Today she is still a growing power even though she is avowedly pacifist. Thus, we must expect that the disparity between her dependence on the United States for defense and her enhanced stature in other respects will continue to grow. The only logical, though not necessarily political, solution to this problem is for her to achieve an autonomous posture in matters of defense as well. The solution is not necessarily political, for two major reasons. One is Japan's own pacifism. However, we must remember that Japan has made two attempts in the past to amend her constitution and put an end to her pacifist character. As I noted in reviewing the trend of Japanese public opinion, it is quite possible that the third challenge against the pacifist regime—administered from without by President Nixon—has set in motion a secular trend that will enable a future LDP prime minister to do what Hatoyama and Kishi tried and failed. That man will be, in fact, founding the second republic.

Or, the second republic may come about in the way predicted here: through the crucible of a national security crisis.

But there is another, much more serious, political obstacle in the way of Japan's assuming an autonomous defense posture: the United States. One of the major purposes of the United States in shouldering the burden of Japan's defense in the postwar period has been, and remains, to control Japan. Japan is kept on a leash because it is assumed that a militarily autonomous Japan would be a destabilizing factor in East Asia, hence inimical to America's interests. Deep in their hearts, the American people cling to the belief that Japan attacked Pearl Harbor without cause and that a militarily autonomous Japan will repeat her past. This is an unfortunate prejudice, though it is not the task of this book to show why.

Japan has always been an insular trading nation that depended —ideally—on a Wilsonian system of free international trade. Of all the countries of the non-Western world, Japan has been the most Western-oriented; she has even been willing to be assimilated into the Western-centered international system. Japan has never had a history of willfully terminating a military alliance with a Western power. It has always been the United States that has initiated the move to cast Japan adrift; thus it was with the Anglo-Japanese alliance that was terminated at American insistence at the Washington Conference of 1922, ultimately driving Japan into the arms of Nazi Germany. So, too, it was with the Japan-U.S. Security Treaty in 1971, which tempted Japan to side with China.

Whether prejudiced or not, the American assumption that a militarily autonomous Japan would be irrational and dangerous was the determining factor in creating a demilitarized and commerce-oriented Japan. To simplify the matter, one can say that America does not know the Japanese in any image other than saber-rattling militarists on the one hand and shrewd merchants indulging in a free ride on American protection on the other.

In the end, the United States has found pacifist and commercial Japan defective and irksome but refuses to countenance a third alternative. Thus, while controlling Japan by means of the alliance, America taunts her about being a "half power" (as in *Three And A Half Powers*, by Harold Hinton) and demands that she end the free ride. The alleged irrationality of Japan's conservative leaders notwithstanding, they know in their bones that of all the powers they must deal with, the United States—with its occasional quixotic inclination and volatile public opinion—would make the most dangerous enemy. And they swallow their pride and do America's bidding.*

In a sense Japan's pacifism is a reflection of the U.S. alliance policy toward her; the United States can be said to have unconsciously colluded with Japan's pacifist left—just as the LDP colluded with it after the 1960 upheaval. Even after the passage of three decades of alliance with Japan—an extraordinary event in history—the United States still cannot quite trust men like Hatoyama, Kishi, Fukuda, and Nakasone, even though they represent the most spirited—in contradistinction to commercial or bureaucratic—part of the Japanese polity and would make the most reliable friends of America. Having experienced the incredible collapse of her mercenary army in Saigon, the United States nevertheless prefers to have an army in Japan whose mission is to fight a holding action until American succor arrives.

---

*A majority of the Americans friendly to Japan would probably regard themselves as friends of the LDP. Do they realize that the LDP's party program, though in abeyance today, upholds constitutional revision and rearmament as the party's goal? Will they desert a friend if she tries to fulfill her old yearning?

But would a militarily autonomous Japan launch herself on a path of imperialism or pose a mortal threat to the United States? Would a nuclear-armed Japan be less reliable than China? Don't America's doubts about a militarily autonomous Japan reflect her uncertainty about her own ability to lead an association of free nations? Why elso would the United States prefer a passive, democratic military dependency to a self-reliant republic willing to come to America's rescue if needed?

In contemplating a militarily autonomous Japan, we should be aware of another vital benefit that is sure to follow. This concerns the problem pointed up by the charge of a "free ride." As I noted earlier, the charge is inaccurate so far as Japan's fiscal contribution to her own defense is concerned. But it does touch on a dimension of the problem that Japan poses to her friends and allies. The charge of a free ride does not imply doubts about Japan's security. It assumes that Japan is enjoying complete external security for free. It is not thereby suggested that Japan should end the free ride by remilitarizing. The suggestion is rather that Japan should keep the free ride but compensate for it by making larger nonmilitary contributions toward the stability and well-being of the world.

This analysis is wholly apolitical because it confounds the cause and effect of Japan's lack of initiative. As long as the Japanese people are content to live with the assumption that Americans will lay down their lives to defend them against external menace, why should they care about a mere imbalance in the U.S. trade accounts, the plight of refugees from tyranny, or the strategic efforts to shore up the peace in Mideast? Japan's military and nonmilitary contributions are not each other's opportunity cost. Japan's nonmilitary contributions and initiatives will increase only when she is allowed to commit herself politically and strategically.

The Japanese Problem arises from the contradiction of her being an unarmed economic giant, and this is to a degree a reflection of the contradiction in U.S. policy toward her. But so long as the American presence in East Asia was dominant, the contradiction did not matter much. The United States could have it both ways with Japan: demanding mutuality in the alliance while obliquely warning against autonomy. But the most pertinent question that is raised today is not whether a militarily autonomous Japan poses a danger to the United States, but whether the United States can go on performing the task of protecting Japan. To say the least, U.S. policy toward Asia has become fluid in the 1970s. The United States threatened to end the alliance with Japan in 1971; she retreated from Vietnam; she has begun withdrawing from South Korea; and she has abandoned Taiwan.

The United States can no longer have it both ways regarding Japan's defense or status. The United States must either offer a reliable guarantee of Japan's security that includes the security of her last outer defense in Korea, or she must allow Japan to shift to a more independent posture. To lull the Japanese with an illusion of security only to awaken them with a rude shock would be to invite serious consequences.

In my opinion, Japan will not try to change her status as a pacifist dependency until and unless such a change is forced on her by a security crisis. Then she is most likely to take the Gaullist alternative. It is inconceivable that Japan would become a communist state except through foreign conquest. There is no more chance that Japan will return to the imperialist- colonialist past than that the United States or Great Britain will do so. In President Nixon's Guam doctrine, he envisioned a Gaullist role for Japan. Such a Japan would be an even stauncher friend of the United States, fully committed to mutual security and protection. A democracy with strong republican inclinations, she would be sharing identical values with America. Economically, technologically, and culturally, she would be no less integrated with the United States than she is today. But she would possess a force de frappe to deter Soviet nuclear blackmail; thus, she would also replace the United States as the dominant power in the western Pacific. In such a world, the United States would possess a one and a half war capability plus Japan.

Such a world may be in the offing, whatever our wishes. Strategic thinkers on both sides of the Pacific ought to give more thought to it, so that the extraordinary friendship between the United States and Japan will continue into the future.

Appendixes

(Unit: ¥1 billion, %)

FY / Item	GNP (initial forecast) (A)	General account (original) (B)	Growth from previous year	Defense budget (original) (C)	Growth from previous year	Ratio of defense budget to GNP (C/A)	Ratio of defense budget to general account (C/B)
1955	7,559.0	991.5	△0.8	134.9	△3.3	1.78	13.61
1960	12,748.0	1,569.7	10.6	156.9	0.6	1.23	9.99
1965	28,160.0	3,658.1	12.4	301.4	9.6	1.07	8.24
1970	72,440.0	7,949.8	17.9	569.5	17.7	0.79	7.16
1971	84,320.0	9,414.3	18.4	670.9	17.8	0.80	7.13
1972	90,550.0	11,467.7	21.8	800.2	19.3	0.88	6.98
1973	109,800.0	14,284.1	24.6	935.5	16.9	0.85	6.55
1974	131,500.0	17,099.4	19.7	1,093.0	16.8	0.83	6.39
1975	158,500.0	21,288.8	24.5	1,327.3	21.4	0.84	6.23
1976	168,100.0	24,296.0	14.1	1,512.4	13.9	0.90	6.22
1977	192,850.0	28,514.3	17.4	1,690.6	11.8	0.88	5.93
1978	210,600.0	34,295.0	20.3	1,901.0	12.4	0.90	5.54

APPENDIX B
Defense Expenditure

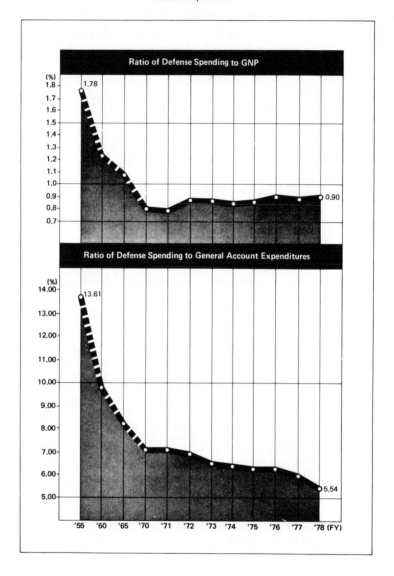

Ratio of Defense Spending to GNP

Ratio of Defense Spending to General Account Expenditures

APPENDIX C
Composition of Defense Expenditure

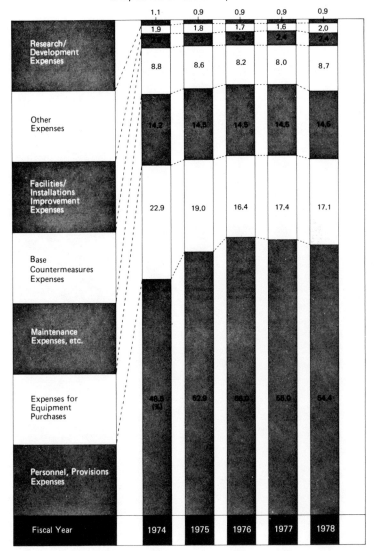

	1974	1975	1976	1977	1978
(top)	1.1	0.9	0.9	0.9	0.9
Research/Development Expenses	1.9	1.8	1.7	1.6	2.0
	2.4	2.5	2.5	2.4	2.4
	8.8	8.6	8.2	8.0	8.7
Other Expenses	14.2	14.5	14.5	14.5	14.5
Facilities/Installations Improvement Expenses	22.9	19.0	16.4	17.4	17.1
Base Countermeasures Expenses					
Maintenance Expenses, etc.					
Expenses for Equipment Purchases	48.5 (%)	52.9	55.0	55.0	54.4
Personnel, Provisions Expenses					
Fiscal Year	1974	1975	1976	1977	1978

Notes

1. Hata Ikuhiko, *Shiroku Nihon saigumbi* [History of Japan's Rearmament] (Tokyo: Bungei Shunju-sha, 1976), p. 74.

2. Martin E. Weinstein, *Japan's Postwar Defense Policy: 1947–1968* (New York: Columbia University Press, 1971), is the best book available on the origin of the Security Treaty, although Weinstein seems to overemphasize the element of freedom that Yoshida is said to have enjoyed.

3. Shimizu Ikutarō, "Koremade no jūnen, kore kara no jūnen" [The past decade, the next decade], *Sekai*, July 1959, pp. 49–50.

4. Tominomori Eiji, *Sengo hoshutō shi* [History of postwar conservative parties] (Tokyo: Nihon Hyōron-sha, 1977), p. 63.

5. The opposition had always lambasted the "unequal" character of the 1951 treaty. But when Kishi turned the tables on it and proposed a treaty revision, the opposition decided for status quo, i.e., keeping the treaty, together with the Peace Constitution.

6. Donald C. Hellman, *Japan and East Asia: The New International Order* (New York: Praeger, 1972). Hellmann characterizes Japan's foreign policy as the "foreign policy of a trading company." Note the similar assessment by Chalmers Johnson in the quotation below.

7. Tominomori, *Sengo hoshutō shi*, p. 144.

8. Chalmers Johnson, "The Japanese Problem," in Donald C. Hellman, ed., *China and Japan: A New Balance of Power* (Lexington, Mass.: Lexington Books, 1976), p. 54.

9. George F. Kennan, *American Diplomacy: 1900–1950* (Chicago: University of Chicago Press, 1951), p. 49.

10. *Mainichi shimbun* (Tokyo), March 9, 1979, morning ed., p. 23.

11. Doi Takeshi, *The Anatomy of Dependence* (Tokyo: Kodansha International, 1973).

12. To cite one example: Dorothy Borg and Okamoto Shumpei, eds., *Pearl Harbor as History: Japanese-American Relations, 1931–1941* (New York: Columbia University Press, 1973).

13. Mainichi Shimbun-sha, *Jimin-tō seiken no anzen-hoshō* [Security policy of the Liberal Democratic government] (Tokyo: Mainichi Shimbun-sha, 1969), pp. 87–88.

14. *Asahi shimbun* (Tokyo), February 4, 1978, morning ed., p. 2.

15. Kurisu Hiro'omi, *The Wing*, January 4, 1978, p. 2.

16. *Asahi shimbun* (Tokyo), July 16, 1979, morning ed., p. 2.

17. Ibid., November 1, 1978, morning ed., p. 2.

18. Kubo Takuya and Shinohara Hiroshi, "Kokumin no tachiba de bōei o minaosu" [Looking at defense from the people's standpoint], *Kokubō*, September 1975, pp. 8–20.

19. Japan, Defense Agency, *Defense of Japan* (Tokyo, 1978), p. 68.

20. Ibid., p. 70.

21. U.S., Department of Defense, *Report of Secretary of Defense Harold Brown to the Congress* (Washington, D.C., January 25, 1979), pp. 50–54, 104–6.

22. Japan, Defense Agency, *Defense of Japan*, p. 69.

24. U.S., Department of Defense, *Report of Secretary of Defense Harold Brown*, p. 105.

25. Alexis de Tocqueville, *Democracy in America* (New York: Random House, 1945), 1: 210.

Index

Airborne early warning, 54
Arab oil embargo, 27
Arendt, Hannah, 23
Ashida Hitoshi, 11, 12

BADGE (Base Air Defense Ground
   Environment) system, 54
"Baroque in our time," 27
Basic Policies for National Defense, 45
Bell, Daniel, 9
Bhutto, Ali, 20
Blockade strategy, 60, 62
Blue Storm Society, 37
Bretton Woods Agreement, 8, 9
Brookings Institution, 61
Brown, Harold (U.S. Secretary of
   Defense), 48, 51, 61
Bureaucrat-politicians, 14, 17

Carter administration, 14, 63
Center parties, 35
"Cheap ride," 31
China, 35, 36, 47, 58–59
Chou En-lai, 27, 47
Clean Government party, 35–36
Communists, see Japan Communist
   party
Conscientious intellectuals, 3, 14
Conservatives, 14, 17, 22, 24–27 passim.
   See also Liberal Democratic party
   and individual prime ministers
   by name

Defense buildup plans, 45, 47, 54
Defense controversy, 32–33, 44–47
"Defense plus," 50

Defensive defense, 30, 39. See also Peace
   Constitution
Democratic Socialist party, 35
Disarmament of Japan, 9–11, 21–22,
   30–31
Domino theory, falling, 25
DSP, see Democratic Socialist party
Dulles, John Foster, 13–14, 15

"Economic animal," 20
Eisenhower, Dwight D., 19
Elections: 1976, 34; 1977, 34; 1979,
   40–41
Emmerson, John K., 23
Emperor of Japan, 10

Falling domino theory, 25
Far Eastern Military Tribunal, 8, 16, 29
Force de frappe, 31, 69
Free ride, 6, 31, 68
Fukuda Takeo (prime minister), 3, 6, 27,
   32, 37, 39, 40–41, 67

Gaullism, 2, 18, 31
Ghetto army, 52
Grumman E2C, 54
Guideline for Japan-U.S. Defense
   Cooperation, 45, 55–56
Guilt, see War guilt

Hata Ikuhiko, 10
Hatoyama Ichirō (prime minister),
   18–19, 66
Hinton, Harold, 67
Holloway, Adm. James (chief of naval
   operations), 61